Currency Trading in the FOREX and Futures Markets

Currency Trading in the FOREX and Futures Markets

Carley Garner

Vice President, Publisher: Tim Moore
Associate Publisher and Director of Marketing: Amy Neidlinger
Executive Editor: Jim Boyd
Editorial Assistant: Pamela Boland
Operations Manager: Jodi Kemper
Senior Marketing Manager: Julie Phifer
Assistant Marketing Manager: Megan Graue
Cover Designer: Chuti Prasertsith
Managing Editor: Kristy Hart
Project Editor: Jovana San Nicolas-Shirley
Copy Editor: Bart Reed
Proofreader: Mike Henry
Indexer: Larry Sweazy
Compositor: Nonie Ratcliff
Manufacturing Buyer: Dan Uhrig

© 2012 by Pearson Education, Inc.
Publishing as FT Press
Upper Saddle River, New Jersey 07458

FT Press offers excellent discounts on this book when ordered in quantity for bulk
purchases or special sales. For more information, please contact U.S. Corporate and
Government Sales, 1-800-382-3419, corpsales@pearsontechgroup.com. For sales
outside the U.S., please contact International Sales at international@pearson.com.

Company and product names mentioned herein are the trademarks or registered
trademarks of their respective owners.

Printed in the United States of America

First Printing January 2012

ISBN-10: 0-13-293137-0
ISBN-13: 978-0-13-293137-3

Pearson Education LTD.
Pearson Education Australia PTY, Limited.
Pearson Education Singapore, Pte. Ltd.
Pearson Education Asia, Ltd.
Pearson Education Canada, Ltd.
Pearson Educatión de Mexico, S.A. de C.V.
Pearson Education—Japan
Pearson Education Malaysia, Pte. Ltd.

The Library of Congress cataloging-in-publication data is on file.

This book is dedicated to DeCarley Trading and its wonderful clients, those by my side with every key stroke (Tracy, Maggie, and Bailey), and those with big dreams as well as the motivation to make them reality. Dream until your dream comes true!

Contents

Contents   ix

Acknowledgments

I'm grateful for my friends and family that exude support and positivity regardless of the circumstances or the geographical distance the pursuit of life has driven between us.

I'd like to thank the crew at FT Press for consistent efficiency and innovation; without their support and entrepreneurial spirit, none of this would be possible.

Most of all, I am humbled by those that sacrifice so much to ensure Americans are provided freedom of expression, the opportunity to seek happiness, and the liberty to chase success without limits.

About the Author

Carley Garner is an experienced futures and options broker and co-owner of DeCarley Trading in Las Vegas, Nevada. She is also the author of *A Trader's First Book on Commodities* and *Commodity Options* published by FT Press. She has contributed to the *FT Press Delivers* line of digital products, *Insights for the Agile Investor*. Her e-newsletters, *The DeCarley Perspective*, *The Stock Index Report*, and *The Bond Bulletin* have garnered a loyal following.

Carley is a Magna Cum Laude graduate of the University of Nevada Las Vegas, where she earned dual bachelor's degrees in Finance and Accounting. She jumped into the options and futures industry with both feet in early 2004 and has become one of the most recognized names in the business.

Throughout her fast-paced career, Carley has been featured in the likes of Stocks & Commodities, Futures, Active Trader, Option Trader, Your Trading Edge, Equities, Expiring Monthly, and Pitnews magazine. Carley is often interviewed by news services, such as Reuters and Dow Jones Newswire, and has been quoted by the *Investor's Business Daily* and *The Wall Street Journal*. She has also participated in radio interviews and can be found on the speaking circuit. Carley is also proactive in providing free trading education; for details, visit www.DeCarleyTrading.com.

Introduction to the World
of Currencies

The concept of currency in civilization dates back to the ancient Egyptians, but the ability for the average individual to participate in the speculation of currency is a relatively new concept. As technology improves, so does the ease of access to the markets; compliments of lower barriers to entry, popularity in currency trading has soared.

Whether or not the inflow of currency speculators to the financial markets throughout the previous decade has had a positive or negative outcome on valuation is still up for debate. Some argue the added market liquidity enables markets to "discover" pricing more efficiently(liquidity is simply the ability to easily enter and exit a market efficiently and is the result of more market participants and higher trading volume).

Others claim overzealous speculators teaming together create illogical, and often unsustainable, price moves. Two things are clear: This is a completely different game than it was 20 years ago, and volatility should be expected. Simply complaining about how things were in the "good ol' days" won't make a dime for anyone; in fact, if you are an Internet FOREX chat room groupie, you might find yourself the target of hate e-mail. A wise trader once told me, you can't control what happens in the markets but you can control how you react to them. I believe that becoming a successful trader means being nimble to changes in market conditions, including the ability to adapt to various shifts in participant psychology and behavior.

> "I didn't fail the test, I just found 100 ways to do it wrong."
> —Benjamin Franklin

As an industry insider who makes a living from retail speculation in both the currency and commodity markets, it is apparent that speculators do have the power to drive market prices beyond equilibrium. Although this has always been the case, it seems to be exaggerated now that there is widespread access to the markets by both the sophisticated and unsophisticated retail traders. That said, prior to the door being opened to retail speculation, dramatic price moves still occurred; however, the cause was likely light volume rather than a bandwagon mentality that now dominates trade. Accordingly, the financial markets will never be perfect because the primary driving force behind them, humans, will never be. Instead, we are emotional and irrational creatures with a tendency to run with the herd toward the slaughterhouse.

As you begin to navigate the currency markets, it is imperative that you understand the difficulty of the task. If using the currency markets as a personal ATM machine were easy, people would quit their day jobs and prepare for a life of luxury. In reality, the statistics suggests that most active currency traders will leave more money in the markets than they walk away with. Similarly, reading a shelf of FOREX books will lay the groundwork for successful trading but certainly doesn't guarantee it. Unfortunately, the most valuable lessons along your journey will be expensive, and will be taught to you by the markets themselves.

As we will cover in detail, low barriers of entry into the currency markets are relatively new; as a result, this particular trading arena has experienced lagging levels of regulation. Consequently, the FX markets have been a hotbed for money laundering, Ponzi schemes, and other types of investor fraud. Whether it is promised trading profits, highly priced educational software that isn't worth the disc it is recorded on, or platforms with flashing green (go) and red (stop) lights indicating "easy" profits from buying or selling currencies, there are plenty of landmines that the average retail currency trader will be forced to tip-toe around. Those who aren't proficient and alert enough to separate truth from fiction could discover the misery aspect of trading before finding success.

The best advice I can offer is to conduct due diligence on each and every trading system, platform, educational course, account manager, and brokerage firm you are considering. Although U.S. regulators have cracked down on what was once the "Wild West" of the financial markets, there are still plenty of traps to fall into.

In addition, traders must have realistic expectations of profit and loss. Many speculators come to the currency markets with dreams of windfall profits, but the reality is much different. In fact, some of the best FX traders in the world struggle to make 20% to 30% per year...and many would be happy with much less. Don't forget, *most* people lose money!

To add perspective to the situation, some of the wealthiest members of our country were begging to be a part of Bernie Madoff's trading program, which was later discovered to be nothing more than a Ponzi scheme. The "expected" return on investment for accounts managed by Madoff was approximately 13% annually.

In other words, if one of the most coveted account managers in the world is only netting 13% for his clients through illegal means, why would the average retail trader approach the market with expectations of double-digit monthly returns? More so, how could FX system and software vendors be promising double-digit *monthly* returns? The reality is, freedom of speech and failing to leave out the entire truth enables FX salesmen to stretch the truth...a lot.

If you are thumbing through a magazine and see claims that are too good to be true, keep flipping because they probably are. Likewise, if you are speaking to a salesperson, whether it is a broker or a software/system representative, and she promises spectacular performance, I suggest hanging up the phone and saving the heartache of discovering the truth the expensive way. If 13% annually was enough to get the uber-rich excited, it should be enough to intrigue all of us, so forget about the triple-digit gains. Even if you are able to make 100% or more in a single year, it is likely you are taking on too much risk and leverage—if so, the fun probably won't last.

My goal isn't to deter anybody from trading FOREX, nor am I insinuating that there isn't money to be made in currency trading. In fact, it is the opposite; however, I also want traders to be realistic in their expectations of risk and reward by acknowledging the difficulty of the task. Without this basic concession, the door is left open for an unpleasant experience. As Charlie Sheen would say, I'm simply delivering "torpedoes of truth."

In reality, the markets can be anything a trader wants them to be. For those looking to substitute a pull at a high-dollar slot machine, there is plenty of leverage available in the currency markets to do just that. On the other hand, the opportunity is there for those seeking the possibility of slow and steady trading profits—

> "If people knew how hard I had to work to gain my mastery, it would not seem so wonderful at all."
> —Michelangelo

assuming enough time is dedicated toward market education, sufficient skin is left in the game to gain experience the only way possible (the hard way), and the trader finds a way to successfully manage emotions and risk.

The currency markets are complex, and adding to the confusion of entry-level speculators is the choice of trading arenas. The most renowned venue to trade currencies is FOREX, or simply FX, but the oldest is currency futures on the Chicago Mercantile Exchange (CME). The new kid on the block, and perhaps the least efficient method of placing wagers on currency fluctuations, is the Exchange Traded Fund (ETF).

Each of these trading arenas has advantages and disadvantages; the purpose of this book is to provide readers with an objective and informative point of view to enable educated decision-making. After all, speculation isn't a "one size fits all" game. What is comfortable and familiar for one trader might be the opposite experience for another. As a trader, it is up to you to determine which avenue of speculation fits your needs and, most importantly, your personality. My hope is that readers are able to walk away with the ability to do just that.

> "Calling someone who trades actively in the market an investor is like calling someone who repeatedly engages in one-night stands a romantic."
> —Warren Buffet

1

What Is FOREX?

The commonly used term FOREX is simply an abbreviation for "foreign exchange." You might also hear this referred to as FX or, as U.S. regulatory bodies refer to it, "retail off-exchange currency market." The FOREX market is a worldwide, decentralized, over-the-counter financial market in which counterparties can facilitate the trading of currencies. The *true* FX market is composed of several electronic communication networks (ECNs) between banks, institutions, and speculators. As you will later learn, not all FOREX brokers provide their clients with access to an actual ECN marketplace; instead, their clients trade in a synthetic environment that merely appears to be a free market.

> The FOREX market is actually a collection of several freestanding markets on completely separate networks and various counterparties.

Unlike equities, or even most futures and options, FX trading does not occur on an exchange floor, nor are trades executed through a common exchange (such as the Chicago Mercantile Exchange or the New York Stock Exchange). Instead, buyers and sellers are facilitating electronic contractual agreements in regard to the exchange of underlying currencies with assorted counterparties and under various arrangements. Accordingly, currency contracts traded in FX are said to be "off-exchange" products.

According to Wikipedia, a **counterparty** is a financial term identifying a party to a contract or agreement. In FOREX, counterparty holds the same definition and is used to refer to any party that executes a buy or sell in the foreign exchange market. This might be a bank, a central bank, a corporation, a speculator, or even *the brokerage firm executing the transaction.*

Although a counterparty can be on either side of the trade, it is most commonly used as a description of the party taking the other side of a retail trader's order. If a trader buys 100,000 worth of the USD/JPY, somebody else has to sell it to her and that somebody is known as the counterparty.

Trades executed in the FX market are known as "spot" transactions. The term **spot** typically refers to an immediate exchange of assets, but in the case of FOREX it is actually a two-day delivery. Therefore, the concept of trading in FOREX is similar to that of futures trading, in which delivery of the underlying asset takes place at a specified time in the future. Nonetheless, the time frames are much different. Whereas FX contracts are deliverable within a few days, futures are often deliverable months in advance.

Also similar to trading futures contracts, a currency trader in FOREX is buying and selling agreements to make or take delivery of the underlying asset at a specific time and date. Nonetheless, speculators are rarely interested in being part of the delivery process and therefore repetitively roll their obligation out into the future until they are ready to exit the position by offsetting their liability with their counterparty.

> A **counterparty** is any person or entity that takes the other side of an agreement. In FOREX, the counterparty might be a bank, institution, broker, or retail trader.

We will later discover that FX brokers automatically roll client positions to avoid the hassles of delivery. Perhaps this is why you don't hear tall tales about FX traders being forced to accept 100,000 Euro like you do about the infamous corn trader who had to store 5,000 bushels on the front lawn.

Beginning traders are often overwhelmed by the concept of selling something before buying it. Because FX traders are exchanging agreements with each other, rather than the actual underlying assets, there is no need to "own" anything before selling. FOREX traders can buy and sell in any order, depending on the direction they believe prices will move. We will discuss the mechanics later, but traders who expect the value of the Euro to depreciate relative to the U.S. Dollar might "go short" (sell) the Euro against the Dollar. A different trader might "go long" (buy) the Euro against the Dollar if she expects the Euro to appreciate; these trades can be made in any order and without regard to any ownership. Whether a trader buys or sells an instrument to enter a speculative position, the exit of the trade can only be accomplished by performing the opposite action in the same quantity of currency.

> FOREX traders are exchanging liabilities, not assets.

FX Swung the Door Open to Currency Volatility

Global ECN markets, collectively referred to as FX, were created to simplify the transfer of assets between businesses, banks, and countries worldwide. Nonetheless, improvements in technology throughout the years and lower barriers to entry have opened the door to a hotbed of speculation. In the beginning, trading was only available to relatively high-net-worth individuals with a certain degree of clout. Today, it is possible to open a micro FX brokerage account in a matter of hours by completing an electronic application; minimum funding requirements for micro FX accounts are as low as a Dollar. Yes, that's right…I said a Dollar. But don't expect to get much done with this—you are likely better off buying a lottery ticket with the money.

> When it comes to the markets, street-smarts trump book-smarts.

I'm not here to judge whether or not the additional liquidity brought by speculators has been a positive for the market place, but in the end, the FOREX market and all of its participants determine the relative value of various currencies in relation to others. With so many opinions being expressed through buying and selling of currency pairs, there are bound to be some intense price moves.

Counterparty Risk

Because there is no official exchange overseeing transactions and clearing FOREX trades, there is also no exchange guarantee. As a result, traders in the FOREX market are exposed to counterparty risk, which is not necessarily the case in stock or futures trading.

In essence, traders exposed to counterparty risk could find themselves in a situation in which they are not entitled to the profits earned on a particular trade should the market maker on the other side of the transaction fail to live up to his end of the bargain. Although, this scenario is extremely rare, it must be acknowledged as a potential risk and considered when choosing a currency trading arena.

FOREX Hours

The very same characteristics of FOREX that make it a unique alternative for speculators also create a complicated and treacherous marketplace for those who aren't fully prepared. For example, the FX markets are available to traders continuously, 24 hours per day, five and a half days a week. Specifically, trading begins at 20:15 GMT on Sunday and ends at 22:00 GMT on Friday. The lack of downtime is convenient and enables traders to react to world events in real time, unlike stock traders, who have to wait for the morning open of the U.S. trading session. Yet, day and night market access also encourages poor sleeping habits by die-hard FX traders, and this could promote unfortunate decision-making and large losses. On a social note, it is also probably the root of many failed marriages.

Although FX is open for trade 24 hours per day, there are certain times at which more trading activity occurs, thus providing favorable market conditions for speculators. Liquidity in the FOREX market travels across the globe with the time zones.

From the perspective of a trader located in the United States, the trading day actually begins the night before in Sydney, Australia at 5:00 p.m. Eastern Standard Time (EST); however, liquidity doesn't tend to show up until the Tokyo open a few hours later. At 3:00 a.m. EST, the London markets open, and finally the U.S. market officially opens at 8:00 a.m. local time in New York City. As you can see in Table 1-1, there is plenty of action around the clock, but that doesn't necessarily mean you should always try to take advantage of it. The most liquidity can be found during the overlapped time between the London and the New York sessions, or approximately 8:00 a.m. to 12:00 p.m. Eastern Standard Time.

Table 1-1 Trading Day Begins with Sydney at 5 p.m. EST and Ends at the New York Close at 5 p.m. EST

FX Trading Hours (Eastern Standard Time)

	1	2	3	4	5	6	7	8	9	10	11	12	1	2	3	4	5	6	7	8	9	10	11	12
Sydney					▓	Sydney	▓	▓	▓	▓	▓	▓	▓	▓										
Tokyo							▓	Tokyo	▓	▓	▓	▓	▓	▓	▓	▓								
London															▓	London	▓	▓	▓	▓	▓	▓	▓	▓
New York	▓	▓	▓	▓	▓															▓	New York	▓	▓	▓

Sydney is open from 5:00 p.m. to 2:00 a.m. EST.

Tokyo is open from 7:00 p.m. to 4:00 a.m. EST.

London is open from 3:00 a.m. to 12:00 EST.

New York is open from 8:00 a.m. to 5:00 p.m. EST.

FOREX Regulation

Once again, FOREX is a comparatively new trading venue for the average retail currency trader, and with new comes a lack of regulation. In recent years, the NFA (National Futures Association) has begun pulling the reins in on FOREX brokerage firms and their practices, but the jurisdiction of U.S. regulators can't, and doesn't, extend beyond domestic borders. Accordingly, as U.S. regulators were scrambling to write, implement, and enforce new rules aimed at protecting the public from misleading or fraudulent activity, traders reacted by opening trading accounts with brokerage firms operating overseas. The jury is still out on whether this global competition is in the best interest of traders; nonetheless, despite a lack of jurisdiction, U.S. authorities are working hard to prevent U.S. traders from using foreign-operated brokerage houses that don't comply with U.S. regulations. In fact, at the time of this writing, it seemed as though most foreign FX brokers were honoring the wishes of U.S. regulators by either refraining from accepting U.S. citizens as clients or operating a branch of their business according to U.S. rules to accommodate U.S. clients.

> U.S. regulators prohibit brokerage firms from granting U.S. clients leverage in excess of 50 to 1, regardless of which country the broker is headquartered.

The Basics of FOREX Margin

Beginning traders often fail to realize that **margin** isn't a cost; instead, it is simply a good-faith deposit required by brokerage firms as collateral to ensure the ability to cover losses suffered in speculative trades. In other words, despite sometimes being called a "margin charge," it isn't a charge at all. You can look at it similar to the down payment banks (should) require for a mortgage loan to cover any possible drawdowns in the value of the home. If a homeowner is required to provide $20,000 as a down payment to qualify for a loan, the balance goes toward equity in the home to be recouped when the home is later sold (assuming it is sold for a higher price than the loan balance). The down payment, similar to FX margin, isn't an expense; instead, it is a buffer against the possibility of lower home values and borrower default. FX margin should be looked at in the same manner.

The popularity of FX exploded once retail traders caught wind of the excessive leverage built into the marketplace, and this didn't take long given the aggressive advertising techniques of the first FOREX brokers on the scene. New regulations put in place by the NFA limit the leverage U.S. brokerage firms can offer to 50 to 1; the original regulatory leverage cap established in 2010 was 100 to 1, but it was quickly restricted even further. In the simplest view, assuming a 50-to-1 leverage ratio, for every Dollar in margin collateral on deposit, a trader can enjoy or suffer from the profits or losses of $50 worth of currency.

> Margins should be looked at as a down payment against possible losses—not as an expense.

Although the NFA limits leverage provided to U.S. FX traders to 50 to 1, some overseas brokerage firms offer much more. In fact, I've seen firms offer leverage to the tune of 400 to 1! On the other hand, the NFA does not stipulate the minimum leverage an FX trader can utilize. This might seem obvious, but traders typically overlook its implication.

Although traders might be free to utilize high amounts of leverage, they can always choose not to by executing trades in smaller volume relative to account size. Leverage can be eliminated altogether by simply funding the account with the entire contract value; also known as the nominal value. In most FX currency pairs (currency futures will be slightly different), this is approximately $100,000 per standard contract, $10,000 per mini contract, and $1,000 per micro. It might appear unproductive to eliminate the leverage, but some of the most successful derivatives traders have done it this way. Realistically, I believe the optimal balance to be somewhere in the middle.

> Good traders know when to take their winnings and run!

For instance, a trader buying or selling a contract valued at $100,000 would need to have $2,000 in a trading account to meet the minimum margin requirement as stated by NFA's 50 to 1 leverage regulation ($100,000/50, or (1/50) × $100,000). The same trader could reduce her leverage, and thus exposure to risk, by either funding the account with much more than the required $2,000 or simply trading a smaller contract size. As we will later discuss, mini FX contracts can be bought and sold in increments of $10,000; accordingly, this trader could opt to trade $10,000 instead of $100,000 with an account size of $2,000. By doing this, she would adjust her leverage ratio to a more comfortable 5 to 1.

Although more government regulation in the financial markets isn't always the best remedy, I was a supporter of the NFA's original leverage cap. 100 to 1 is more than enough for speculators; in my opinion, anything more is the equivalent to the Shards O' Glass popsicles in the "Truth" ads speaking out against tobacco. Further, I believe aggressive marketing of high leverage is unethical in that it promotes low-probability trading and breeds anguish, for the sake of generating massive brokerage revenue. Unfortunately, higher rates of leverage are easy to sell to novice traders because newcomers tend to look at trading with a glass-half-full mentality; they have a propensity to focus on the positive and block out the negative. I rarely hear a beginning trader ask how to calculate the amount of money he might lose if the market goes from point A to point B. Instead, I'm routinely asked how much one will *make* if....

It is certainly true that more access to free leverage might translate into faster and larger profits, but the reality of the situation is that it will probably lead to nearly immediately devastating results. In essence, the more leverage a trader uses, the less room for error he is giving himself. When it comes to trading, or anything else in life, the further from perfect you have to be, the better the odds of success you will face.

> FX margin fluctuates with the notional value (total value) of the contract traded and currency valuations if the USD is not the quote currency.

Unfortunately, nothing in FOREX is simple; despite the leverage ratio being stated and constant, the actual margin charge quoted in U.S. Dollars is not. Simply put, margin rates on each currency pair constantly fluctuate in real time with market prices. This differs greatly from trading in the futures markets, where a stated margin rate is relatively stable and standard.

The exact amount brokerage firms expect to be on deposit to hold positions in the FOREX markets is based on the stated leverage ratio (typically the NFA's 50 to 1), the notional value of the holdings (total value of the currency contracts traded), and possibly the exchange rate of the greenback. This is because FOREX traders stand to benefit or suffer from price movements based on the entire value of the trade, the notional value, and not the margin on deposit. Once again, this can be compared to the way home owners are exposed to the price risk of their *entire* property value rather than the down payment and accumulated equity.

Stock traders wishing to trade on leverage, or sell shares short, must first borrow shares from their brokerage firm and pay interest on the loan. Conversely, FOREX traders are buying and selling an agreement to deliver the underlying asset, rather than the asset itself. Therefore, there is no borrowing of currency to initiate a position valued at as much as 50 times the required margin deposit. As mentioned, a FOREX trader is simply required to deposit a down payment on future losses known as margin.

The practice of holding margin, in lieu of the freedom to buy or sell contracts in any order and on leverage, is similar to trading in the futures market but is in stark contrast to the policy of stock brokerage firms. However, in futures it is primarily the exchange that sets margin requirements; the broker plays a secondary role in doing so, and the NFA has yet to establish leverage rules in the futures arena. In Chapter 2, "Making 'Cents' of Currency Pairs," we discuss how FOREX margin is calculated, and in Chapter 6, "What Are Currency Futures?," we cover the details of margin on futures contracts.

> FX and futures traders can trade long or short on leverage without paying interest to their brokerage. This is because, unlike trading stocks, they are trading agreements, not assets.

Despite interest-free leverage provided by brokerage firms, FX traders are subject to the interest rate differential between the currencies in any pair held overnight (beyond the NY close). A position will either earn, or incur, interest depending on the money market rates backing the corresponding currencies. This is unique to currency speculation in FOREX and does not apply to currency futures or ETFs. We will revisit this concept in more detail, but it is important that traders are aware of all the risks, rewards, and liabilities that come with trading spot market currencies.

Market Liquidity: Myths Versus Truths

The appeal of trading liquid markets is the ease with which contracts can be bought and sold, but traders aren't always getting what they expect. You have probably read, or heard, that the foreign currency market is the deepest and most liquid marketplace in the world. Daily FX volume is estimated to be approximately $4 trillion, dwarfing all other speculative vehicles and essentially doubling in size over the last decade. However, the headline figures are a bit misleading. For instance, the daily volume isn't entirely composed of spot transactions by retail speculators, hedge funds, or even banks. Most of it is occurring in forward contracts and foreign exchange swaps; a smaller percentage of the daily volume occurs in options and other peripheral products. Swaps are actions taken by FX traders to avoid delivery of the underlying asset.

> Any product in any market has two prices: one at which it can be bought and one at which it can be sold. The **bid** is the price at which a trader can sell, and the **ask** is the price at which a trader can buy. There will always be a spread between these prices, known as the **bid/ask spread**, or **pip spread**.

Specifically, an **FX swap** is the simultaneous purchase and sale of identical amounts of one currency for another with two different value dates. In a nutshell, it is the process of rolling from a deliverable currency position into a nondeliverable contract; later, we will touch on the concept of rolling over again in more detail. A **forward contract** is an individually negotiated agreement to buy or sell a particular currency at an agreed-upon price and on an agreed-upon date. Neither swaps, nor forwards, add to the liquidity of intraday speculative currency trading. As a result, although they add to the impressiveness of liquidity stats, the stats are a bit misleading.

Even more disingenuous is the assumption that trading FOREX under any brokerage firm, or arrangement, entails enjoying deeply liquid currency markets. Depending on the brokerage firm chosen, trades might not be taking place in a liquid FX market, known as an ECN (Electronic Currency Network). Brokers that provide clients with direct access to an ECN market are known as **non-dealing desk brokers.** On the other side of the coin, brokers that are not routing client orders to an ECN are essentially executing orders in a synthetically created (replica) market. This type of brokerage arrangement is known as a **dealing-desk broker**, and in this environment the broker's "dealing desk" is taking the other side of their client's transactions. We will discuss the details and disadvantages of this later on, but it is important to realize that those trading through a dealing desk aren't directly benefiting from the liquidity in the true FX markets (ECNs). Even those trading in an ECN environment should know that volume is split among several networks rather than a single market. In my view, reporting an aggregate daily FX volume figure as is commonly done can be compared to combining all the volume incurred in each stock exchange around the globe and then claiming the "stock market" is exceptionally liquid.

> We don't compile all the volume executed worldwide and claim the "stock market" is the deepest market in the world, so why do we do it in FOREX? True liquidity can only be measured in each of the individual FX networks.

Each FX pair is quoted in two prices: The bid is the price traders can sell and the ask is the price traders can buy. Unfortunately, the spread between the two is always at the disadvantage of the retail trader. The more liquid the market is, the less distance between the best available bid and the best available ask, which results in better fill quality. Those trading against their brokerage firm are operating in an arrangement where the spreads between the bid (the best price at which you can sell) and the ask (the best price at which you can buy) are fixed. In the case of fixed spreads, it really doesn't matter how liquid or illiquid the FX market is because these traders won't reap any of the benefits!

Nonetheless, even in light of these clarifications on FX market volume, FOREX traders typically enjoy ample liquidity for normal speculation. That said, I believe knowing the big picture will enable traders to make better decisions when choosing a trading arena or environment (that is, a broker).

2

Making "Cents" of Currency Pairs

n FX, a **currency pair** is composed of two elements known as a base currency and a quote currency. The base currency is listed first and the quote currency second, with a hyphen or backslash separating the two. Given this explanation, it isn't difficult to understand why some refer to the base currency as the "primary currency" and the quote currency as the "secondary currency." As mentioned in Chapter 1, "What Is FOREX?," FX currency pairs are most often traded in 100,000 or 10,000 units of the base currency, but some firms offer increments of 1,000. Because size is relatively standard, the FX community often refers to the various contract sizes as a full-sized contract (standard lot), a mini contract, and a micro contract, respectively.

> In FOREX, currencies are like shoes—you can't buy or sell just one!

The term **pair** isn't a coincidence; despite the fact that there are two components to every pair, it is treated as a single instrument or package. Similar to shoes, which can't be bought or sold individually, all currencies must be traded in pairs; in essence, traders are buying one currency and selling the other.

Fundamentally, a pair can be viewed as a single exchange rate with a specific value, but when broken apart the worth of each component is ambiguous and essentially "unquotable." For example, we know that a U.S. Dollar is worth about two candy bars, a pack of gum, or a fountain soda, but without having an asset to compare its value, a Dollar probably isn't worth the paper it is printed on.

Even though it is an uncommon perception, every transaction between two parties involves the purchase of one asset or service and the sale of another. In the days of bartering, this fact was a little more obvious, but in today's world of fiat currency the concept still applies. For instance, if you buy a gallon of milk at the grocery store,

> Currencies only have value relative to something else. When standing alone, they are "unquotable."

you are selling Dollars to purchase milk; similarly, the store is selling its milk to "purchase" Dollars. In this sense, currency pairs in FX are no different from any other aspect of the economy, because it is only possible to measure the value of one item relative to the other. To clarify, the only way to express the value of a gallon of milk is relative to a Dollar or some other asset. Without this relative comparison, it is impossible to quote its value.

The concept of trading a pair can be overwhelming for those not familiar with it, but the key is to understand that the buying or selling of the pair is relative to the base currency. Simply put, the base currency (listed first in the pair) is the one you will be buying or selling, and the quote currency (listed second in the pair) will provide a relative value. Thus, by default, a position opposite of that in the base currency will result in the quote currency. Therefore, if you buy the base currency, you are simultaneously selling the quote currency.

For instance, the most commonly traded FX pair is the EUR/USD (stated as "Euro Dollar"). In this pair, the Euro is the base currency and the U.S. Dollar is the quote currency. If a trader purchased the pair, he would be buying the Euro and selling the Dollar. For example, if a trader bought the EUR/USD at $1.3275, he is paying $1.3275 for each Euro. Naturally, the Euro will have a different value against the Dollar than it might have against the Yen, or any other currency; therefore, the only way to measure the value of the Euro is to relate it to an alternative currency.

On a side note, the term **currency pairs** should not be confused with **currency crosses**, which are special types of currency pairs in that they lack the trader's home currency. Accordingly, for retail FX traders in the U.S., an example of a currency cross would be the GBP/JPY or the EUR/AUD. Likewise, the USD/JPY would *not* be a currency cross because the USD is a component.

Calculating Leverage and Margin

We have discussed that FX brokers in the U.S. are limited in the amount of leverage they can offer as the result of NFA rules capping the leverage ratio at 50 to 1. However, we have not discussed the corresponding margin rate and how it is derived. In other words, the NFA specifies a leverage ratio, but the actual margin required to be on deposit fluctuates with the market—more specifically, the notional value of the trade. If you recall, the notional value is the total value of the currency contract being traded, or the amount of money that would be required if leverage wasn't available.

> The base currency always trumps the quote currency (which is why it is listed first in the pair). It is the one that is bought or sold and is used to determine notional value.

As a reminder, the concept of notional value and margin in FX is similar to the value of a home relative to a down payment. The notional value of the property is the total worth of the home and the fluctuation in this value determines the profit and loss to the buyer. Yet, the homebuyer is only required to put a deposit of 20% down to acquire the property, which is far less than the notional value of the asset.

In FOREX, a leverage ratio of 50 to 1 means that you can buy or sell $100,000 worth of currency while maintaining a margin balance of just $2,000 in your account. Because market prices fluctuate, so does the notional value of each currency pair. Accordingly, the actual margin requirement in FX is variable rather than fixed and will almost never be a round figure such as $2,000.

> "There seems to be some perverse human characteristic that likes to make easy things difficult."
> —Warren Buffet

As if this weren't confusing enough, because two currencies are involved in each pair, there are potentially two relative notional values (one in each currency). Luckily, it is standard to use the base currency to determine the notional value.

For example, if a trader buys 10,000 EUR/USD at $1.3275, the notional value of the trade will be $13,275 (10,000 × $1.3275). If the same trader purchases another 90,000 EUR/USD at the same price, he is said to

---

be long a standard lot (100,000) and will be holding a position with a notional value of $132,750 (100,000 × $1.3275). Keep in mind that U.S. brokerage firms offer leverage of 50 to 1; accordingly, a trader could hypothetically purchase 10,000 Euro at $1.3275 and experience the gains or losses of the notional value ($13,275) with as little as $265.50 in a trading account (that is, (1/50) × 13,275). Likewise, a trader holding 100,000 of the underlying currency will benefit or suffer from price fluctuations of $132,750 worth of Euro with as little as $2,655. It is easy to see how leverage of this magnitude can quickly work both in favor of or against a trader.

The Nuts and Bolts of Trading FX Pairs

Beginning FX traders are often overwhelmed by the logistics of currency trading simply because the concept of buying and selling in any order is foreign to most; in this situation it is complicated by the fact that each contract has two components (a base currency and a quote currency). After all, if all trades involve buying one currency and selling another, how do you know which you are buying and which you are selling when placing an order on the pair?

Once again, the currency in the pair that is bought or sold is the base currency, also known as the primary currency, and is listed first in the pair. Therefore, the opposite action is taken in the other component of the pair by default.

This isn't unlike anything else in life…it is just displayed a little differently. However, the question for many beginning FOREX traders remains: How do brokers know which currency to list as the base currency (first in the pair) and the quote currency (second in the pair)?

The answer is simple: In the world of foreign exchange, the manner in which currency pairs are traded and quoted is relatively standard. To clarify, regardless of the brokerage firm you choose, most of the currency pairs will be identified in the same manner; trading platforms and quotes will always show the EUR/USD and will never show the pair inversely (USD/EUR). Therefore, speculators taking a position in either the Euro or the Dollar will trade the Euro Dollar pair (EUR/USD) as a vehicle.

The standard used to formulate currency pairs for trading is accepted based on the priorities attributed to each currency. Originally, the rank was determined by relative value with respect to each other and on a first-come, first-served basis (simply, they are grandfathered in). However, the advent of the Euro has broken the proverbial unwritten rules. From its inception in 1999, the Euro has had first precedence as a

> An accepted standard determines a priority for formulating pairs. This priority determines which currency is listed as the primary in the pair.

base currency and is, therefore, listed as the first currency in each pair it is a part of. You might be surprised to find the U.S. Dollar in the middle of the priority pack, but that is because we are a relatively new nation and the Dollar a newer currency. Here is a list of the established priority rankings by major currency:

- Euro
- British Pound
- Australian Dollar
- New Zealand Dollar
- U.S. Dollar
- Canadian Dollar
- Swiss Franc
- Japanese Yen

Knowing the order of priority tells us that the Euro versus the Pound will always be the EUR/GBP within FX trading platforms, and the U.S. Dollar versus the Canadian Dollar will always be USD/CAD.

Once you understand that all pairs will *always* be quoted in the same manner (but obviously not at the same price), it is easier to grasp the concept of trading the pair. For instance, if a trader is bearish the U.S. Dollar, he wouldn't be able to sell a USD/EUR pair, but he could buy the Euro against the Dollar and accomplish the same feat (that is, go long the EUR/USD). Again, when buying the EUR/USD, the trader is purchasing the Euro and selling the Dollar simultaneously.

In the case of the Yen versus the Dollar, traders are able to speculate on currency valuations through the USD/JPY pair, or simply the Dollar/Yen. Later in the book, we discuss the unique nature of the Yen in regard to quoting and calculating. If the currency markets were a bus, the Yen would be the "crazy" person your mother warned you about.

Sticking to the Majors

In the world of currency trading, a handful of pairs tend to attract a majority of trading interest; the most active currency pairs are typically referred to as the "majors." Because they attract liquidity, the majors offer traders the freedom of easy entry and exit in the form of narrow bid and ask spreads. Additionally, ample liquidity provides an environment in which less slippage is likely to occur comparative to trading in pairs that are not part of this group. In theory, larger trading volume *should* reduce the amount of intraday volatility, or market noise, but that isn't always the case. In my opinion, because the majors are highly targeted instruments by speculators there are times the added speculation creates *larger* price moves than what might have been the case otherwise. That said, overly speculative price changes are often temporary. If speculators jump on a particular bandwagon, the "bus" will eventually get too full, thus triggering a large counter-trend move. Generally, after prices significantly overshoot the fundamental equilibrium price, they often revert back toward the mean to achieve a more sustainable price level.

Most beginning FOREX traders should primarily trade the "majors." The "minors" pose additional obstacles to traders that arise from a lack of liquidity.

Most of the major currency pairs involve the U.S. Dollar, denoted as USD, against other common currencies such as the British Pound, Swiss Franc, Japanese Yen, and the Euro. Others that aren't quite as liquid but are still labeled in the "Major" category are the Canadian, Australian, and New Zealand Dollars versus the U.S. Dollar.

It seems logical that the group of currency pairs that are not categorized as "majors" are classified as "minors." These pairs often suffer from a lack of liquidity to varying degrees. For example, the USD/MXN (U.S. Dollar versus Peso) pair is thinly traded but is probably going to be much more liquid than the USD/CLP (U.S. Dollar versus Chilean Peso). The more exotic the pair, the thinner it will be…and the thinner it gets the more the odds will be stacked against the trader. It is normally a good idea to avoid trading minor currency pairs, unless of course you strongly believe there is an opportunity that has the potential, and supportive probability, to overcome the difficulties that come with trading illiquid contracts.

FOREX Simplified

Imagine the chaos in the financial markets if asset classifications weren't standardized. For the sake of time, convenience, and clarity, equities and mutual funds are identified with standardized ticker symbols, futures with contract symbols and months, and, finally, FX with standard three-letter identifiers. As a result, traders around the globe, regardless of origin, ethnicity, or language, know exactly what they are buying or selling through a FOREX trading platform.

In the case of FX, we can thank the ISO (International Organization for Standardization) for assigning each currency, or country, with a three-letter abbreviation. This was originally done to facilitate communications and transactions between banks and counterparties, but has now become a well-known language to currency speculators.

The first two letters of the three are the country code, as identified by the ISO; the third letter is usually the initial of the currency itself. For instance, USD stands for United States Dollar and GBP stands for Great Britain Pound. Here is a list of the major currency pairs listed by the ISO codes, as denoted within a FOREX trading platform:

- **EUR/USD**—Euro versus U.S. Dollar
- **GBP/USD**—British Pound versus U.S. Dollar
- **USD/JPY**—U.S. Dollar versus Japanese Yen
- **USD/CHF**—U.S. Dollar versus Swiss Franc
- **USD/CAD**—U.S. Dollar versus Canadian Dollar
- **AUD/USD**—Australian Dollar versus U.S. Dollar
- **NZD/USD**—New Zealand Dollar versus U.S. Dollar

3

FX Brokers and the Reality of
Transaction Costs

Y our trading experience will be directly tied to the type of brokerage firm you use. There is much more to making money in FOREX than being able to forecast price changes, although that is a great start. Choosing the type of FX brokerage, and the particular shop itself, could be the difference between a happy conclusion to your trading journey and the opposite scenario. Not only are there various arrangements for counterparty execution, but there are alternative methods of charging and collecting transaction costs.

Two types of retail FX brokers offer speculative currency trading to investors: traditional brokers that provide clients access to an ECN and brokers that operate as dealing desks.

ECN FX Brokers (Non-Dealing Desk)

Earlier in the book you learned that an ECN is an electronic communication network in which currency pairs are traded by banks, central banks, corporations, and now speculators. ECN brokers, however, are also known as **non-dealing-desk brokers** because, similar to the traditional sense of a broker, they serve as an agent to provide customer access to the FX market (an ECN) as opposed to dealing the FX pairs directly to their clients by acting as a counterparty. ECN brokers are nothing more than the intermediary that brings speculators to liquidity providers (banks and other counterparties). In essence, they attempt to find the best price for the retail trader and facilitate/execute orders on their behalf. Don't forget that there are several ECNs, and the brokerage firm you choose will determine the quality and size of the

ECN. Therefore, bids and asks, and the spread between, can vary from broker to broker.

Retail traders opting for a non-dealing-desk broker will enjoy direct access to a true currency market, and the quotes they see within their platform represent the lowest price at which other participants are willing to sell and the highest price at which they are willing to buy. It might be easier to understand this by thinking of it this way: When you look at quotes flashing on the FX trading platform of a trader using an ECN broker, you see the best offer (ask) and the best bid of all available counterparties on the ECN.

ECN brokers don't "deal" currencies to their clients; instead, they introduce clients to a network of counterparties that they wouldn't otherwise have access to as a means of providing liquidity.

It is the broker that provides access to the marketplace; but it is the trader who determines when and where to buy or sell via the simple click of a button. As you will learn, this arrangement is in stark contrast to those trading with a dealing-desk broker, or non-ECN broker. These traders are faced with the best prices at which *their broker* is willing to execute their trades. As you might have caught on, when you are trading with a non-ECN broker, the brokerage firm takes the other side of your trade. Later we will discuss the conflicts of interest that arise in trading through such a broker.

Currency quotes displayed by a non-dealing-desk broker are the result of the best available prices in a fully functioning free market.

Commission

A nearly unlimited number of FX advertisements claim no-commission trading. However, as a broker who makes a living through commission in both futures and FX, I can tell you that traders are always paying transaction costs in one way or another; nobody works for free.

The goal of trading is to *make* money, not to *save* it! If the pennies you are pinching aren't helping your bottom line enough to keep your account in the black, you should rethink your strategy.

The manner in which transaction costs are charged by brokers and paid by FX traders is highly dependent on the type of brokerage firm chosen. Non-dealing-desk brokers charge a set commission quoted in "per million" traded (you might also see this as "per MIO") for providing clients access to ECN counterparties. Perhaps because the growth of speculation in FOREX can largely be attributed to the idea of commission avoidance, brokerage firms opted to use a less obvious term to describe the fees charged for their services. In the FX industry, this commission is known as a **markup.**

Just like commission rates in futures and equities differ among brokers and service levels, there is some variation in the markup charged by FX firms. Firms commonly charge $100 per million traded; this equates to a $10 markup for a standard contract of $100,000 and $1 per mini, or $10,000 traded.

As a broker in the futures and FOREX industries, I am very aware of the tendency of traders to want to avoid commission charges at all cost. In fact, I'm often reminded that the bulk of traders get so caught up in the idea of finding the cheapest brokerage firm that they forget the goal is to *make* money, not to *save* it. Believe me when I tell you, there is a difference. If you are trading at the absolute lowest possible transaction cost, but you are still losing money, you haven't really done yourself any favor. Even worse, part of the problem might be that you are getting what you pay for.

> FOREX ECN brokerage markups are levied on a per-side basis, rather than round turn, which is customary with futures brokers.

You shouldn't base your decision to trade, or not to trade, with any firm based on the markup alone. If you are paying a little more in transaction costs for access to a quality ECN, valuable market guidance, or a knowledgeable staff, it is money well spent. In fact, paying a reasonable commission or markup is a lot cheaper than paying for unnecessary market mistakes or hidden costs.

Dealing-Desk FX Brokers (Non-ECN)

Again, I believe that a majority of the exponential growth experienced in speculative FOREX trading can be attributed to the marketing efforts of brokerage firms exploiting what they've called commission-free trading. Despite their success in luring traders into the arena, commission-free

---

trading is simply a ploy to redesign the transaction costs structure found in other financial markets and disguise, as well as rename, the fee paid to brokerage firms. Although the industry is quickly transforming, in the not-too-distant past the primary business model of FX brokers in the U.S. was to act as a dealing desk—and traders flocked at the opportunity to be a part of it.

Unlike ECN brokers that simply bring buyers and sellers together, dealing-desk brokers go beyond facilitating the transaction. They actually participate it in by "dealing" trades to clients and taking the other side of the execution. Plainly, if you are trading with a dealing-desk brokerage firm, when you go short a currency pair, the desk goes long. As a result, such brokerage firms are often referred to as **market makers.**

Clients trading with a dealing desk are partaking in an environment that merely mimics an actual FX market. In reality, it isn't a free market at all.

Ironically, many of the brokerage firms acting as market makers immediately offset the risk of taking the other side of client trades by executing an equal and opposite trade in an ECN market in which tighter bid and ask spreads are available. In essence, they are entering nearly no-risk transactions by offering their clients execution at spreads wider than that of the ECN they are using to hedge risk exposure created by making a market for their client. Accordingly, the favorable execution they receive in the ECN guarantees the broker profits from the difference in the spread.

These non-ECN brokers are essentially acting as the counterparty to their own clients in a synthetically created market that merely mimics that of the actual foreign exchange market. Not only is there no exchange, but in the case of this type of brokerage firm relationship, there really isn't a market either. It is just the client versus the house.

In other words, clients of such firms are not participating in the massively liquid markets they have read about and that brought them to FX in the first place. Instead, they are provided with quotes that are merely *tied to* the true FX market. Unlike with actual ECN trades, the counterparty on the other side isn't a bank, a business, or even another trader…it is just the client's broker.

To recap, the price displayed in the trading platform of a non-ECN broker is the price at which the dealing desk is willing to execute a transaction. Unlike an ECN broker, which will show you the best working offer and best working bid of all its liquidity providers, a non-ECN broker displays two prices at which *it* would be willing to execute. Naturally, as a retail trader, you will always be forced to buy at the higher price and sell at the lower price—and this is how dealing desks make their money. Of course, the prices the dealing desk will execute will be worse than the prices you might get through an ECN transaction because the motives are different.

Those taking the other side of your trades in the ECN market are typically speculative, or based on some business or banking need. On the other hand, the brokerage firm taking the other side of non-ECN transactions is primarily looking to profit from the difference between the price it displays as the bid and the price it displays as the ask. A client who simultaneously buys and sells an FX contract would lose the difference between the two prices; the brokerage firm would gain the same amount (ignoring any possible hedges implemented by the broker in an ECN).

This spread between the bid and ask is referred to as the **pip spread** and enables non-ECN brokerage firms to generate revenue for their execution services without charging a traditional commission. We will go into the concept of a pip in more detail, but in its simplest form it is the minimum price movement of a particular currency pair. For instance, if the EUR/USD moves from $1.4202 to $1.4201, it is said to have fallen by 1 pip.

Once more, dealing-desk brokerage firms make money by charging a fixed bid/ask spread, or a pip spread, rather than a transparent commission charge. The pip spread charged to traders at a dealing-desk brokerage firm is considerably wider than the institutional spreads offered on an ECN. As a result, although the transaction costs are hidden in that they are not accounted for as a deduction on the client's statement, they are substantial and shouldn't be overlooked.

Cynics of ECN brokers (mainly dealing desks trying to attract clients) point out the drawback of a markup. Nevertheless, the markup charged by an ECN broker is similar to a membership fee paid to a discount warehouse in that it enables traders to buy and sell pairs at better prices than would otherwise be the case. Accordingly, just as many businesses categorize the annual Costco or Sam's Club membership fee as a necessary expense to eventually cut costs, traders should focus on the total financial burden of trading and not just the obvious expenditures.

Likewise, in my opinion, the idea of trading through a non-ECN broker can be viewed as playing cards with a dealer (the broker) who can see your entire hand. Not only do I believe this practice stacks the odds against clients of dealing-desk brokerage firms, but I argue that it also increases the trader's overall transaction cost per trade.

Traders with accounts at FOREX firms acting as a dealing desk are provided brokerage statements in which there are no visible commissions charged; however, just like casinos in Las Vegas aren't built on winners, FOREX brokers aren't providing a free service. Vegas locals realize that the largest and most expensive casinos on the strip have "tighter" machines than the smaller local casinos, or the older operations in the downtown area. Gamblers from out of town might not realize it, but they are paying for the luxurious atmosphere in the form of lower payout percentages on slot machines. The business of FOREX brokering isn't much different. If you have ever been to a trader's exposition, you know that some of the biggest and most expensive booths in the exhibit hall are representing FX brokers with dealing desks—and this isn't a coincidence.

Pros and Cons of Each Brokerage Type

There are clear distinctions between trading with an ECN broker and a non-ECN broker (market maker). As a trader, it is up to you to determine which venue will be best for your circumstances. In my opinion, traders are best served by being a part of a true spot currency market, and this access can only be provided by ECN brokers. After all, taking part in a unnaturally created market is a lot like sports betting with an undercover and unknown bookie at the local bar as opposed to a "legitimate" operation such as in a Las Vegas sports book. There are certain enhanced risks, and in my view this skews the odds of success in the wrong direction.

Conflict of Interest

The dealing-desk arrangement, or non-ECN broker, creates a significant conflict of interest between the trader and the brokerage simply because the brokerage firm stands to make money as its client loses, and vice versa. This is a rather simplistic view because dealing desks typically offset their market risk by taking the opposite position in an actual interbank market, but you get the idea. If you are a buyer of the USD/JPY and your broker is the seller, the entity you have essentially hired to facilitate your FOREX trading is benefiting from your misery and suffering from your victory. I can't think of any compelling arguments suggesting this arrangement is conducive to the success of traders.

A glaring example of what might go wrong with such an arrangement was made public in August of 2011. The NFA levied a $2,000,000 monetary sanction against one of the most popular dealing-desk FX brokerage firms in the U.S.—FXCM. In addition to the fine, FXCM was ordered to refund approximately $520,000 to customers in which the NFA had discovered the firm benefited from slippage in client execution. The NFA's complaint cited that although FXCM's trading platform offered a "Market at Best" execution button (equivalent to a market order but with a touch of marketing appeal), the broker was not giving clients the best possible fill as was portrayed. According to findings, FXCM offset nearly all of its price risk in an ECN and only reported customer fills *after* it has obtained a fill for itself at the price the client desired or better. Simply, in order for the client's order to be filled, FXCM's order to offset its own risk must have been filled first. Computer trading is fast, but so are markets, and the inevitable delay in client execution seems like a legitimate reason to avoid such a brokerage arrangement. In the event that FXCM was able to obtain a better-than-expected fill for its own benefit in an ECN market (positive slippage), it would not provide clients with the appropriately better fill. This practice was made worse by the fact that FXCM did pass negative slippage to the client.

> Markets magnify personality flaws in traders and bring out the worst in everyone.

Monetary Considerations

Aside from the absence of the conflict of interest seen in a dealing-desk arrangement, there are potential monetary advantages to trading with a non-dealing-desk firm. Because such firms offer traders of all types and sizes access to a true foreign exchange market, they are also able to offer what are known in the business as **institutional spreads,** which are free-floating competitive bids and asks that vary with liquidity.

During active parts of the day, the spreads will be at their narrowest point, and during slower times of the day, they will be a bit wider. Floating bid/ask spreads are the norm in any market, but they are *not* a part of the synthetically created markets dealing desks offer because the trading environment is not a true marketplace with multiple buyers and sellers. Although a bid/ask spread will always exist in any market, even for those using a non-dealing desk-brokerage, it is an exaggerated obstacle for those trading with a dealing-desk broker. This is because, as we know, they charge their clients a fixed (nonvariable) pip spread above and beyond what the actual interbank market prices are.

Wide pip spreads directly reduce the profits and increase the losses of every trade, just as a more traditional commission charge would. Additionally, the lack of transparency in transaction costs with a dealing desk could encourage overtrading, and the hidden cost is often higher than a markup might be after one considers the differences in fill quality.

Price Manipulation

Again, dealing-desk brokers have the propensity to directly benefit from their client's peril. Hence, traders who experience market losses find an easy scapegoat in the fact that their brokerage firm could be intentionally spiking prices to run stop-loss orders, or worse. Such a practice is difficult to prove and in most instances probably doesn't occur. Nonetheless, the risk is there, and as a trader you don't want to put yourself in a situation where others can be blamed for your failures. Simply put, whether or not dealing desks act with integrity is irrelevant; if you are going to constantly question if something unjust is happening, you shouldn't be trading with a non-ECN brokerage house.

Among the practices some dealing desk brokers are guilty of is **requoting**, which involves a dealing-desk broker filling an order at a price not seen on their public price feed. For example, a trader who enters an order to purchase 100,000 EUR/USD at the market based on an ask quote of 1.4250 but gets filled at 1.4253 has experienced a requote. In the futures and stock markets, this is known as **slippage** and is a normal cost of trading, despite being annoying. Even though traders have one-click electronic market access, it is entirely possible for prices to change as the trade is being placed. For instance, if an order is entered to buy a currency pair at the ask, the ask might change in the split-second it takes to click the mouse. A way to avoid the possibility of a requote is to enter a limit order to buy at the ask, or for bears an order to sell at the bid, or somewhere in between. Doing so doesn't guarantee a fill, but it does guarantee a price. Order types are discussed in detail in Chapter 7, "Calculating in Currency Futures."

I'm not going to judge whether requoting is right or wrong, but it is fair to say that requoting tends to occur much more frequently when it is an advantage to the brokerage firm and a disadvantage to the client. Keep in mind, however, this is typically only seen during fast market conditions and for those trading larger contract sizes. In all fairness, brokers that are acting as the counterparty must have the ability to requote in order to continue functioning profitably; traders shouldn't expect their brokers (dealing desks), assuming they are otherwise acting with integrity, to "eat" all of the price slippage during volatile market conditions. After all, traders in any other arena wouldn't expect this from their trade execution, regardless of who is on the other side of the transaction.

You might also run across the concept of **ballooning pip spreads**, which involves market makers expanding the pip spreads (the spread between the bid and ask) shown to clients during fast, illiquid, or unpredictable markets. For instance, immediately preceding the announcement of an important piece of economic data, dealing desks might look to mitigate their risk of taking the other side of client trades by increasing the price at which they are willing to sell as well as decreasing the price at which they are willing to buy. Naturally, by doing this they are simultaneously unfavorably shifting the prices their clients are subject to by increasing the price their clients must pay to buy a currency pair and decreasing the price at which their clients can sell.

This might sound sneaky, but once again, this isn't unusual in the financial markets. Market makers in the options or futures markets often behave in the same manner, but because they are anonymous, and not the brokerage firm itself, traders typically don't let it bother them. Market makers of all types are providing a service, and they deserve to be compensated. Therefore, if widening spreads to mitigate risk is necessary to stay in the black, so be it. Market makers only make money if trades are executed, but just like traders, if the risk in doing so outweighs the reward, they should have the option to protect themselves. If your brokerage firm does this, you have the choice of opting against trading at such times or trying an ECN brokerage firm. In an ECN environment, there are several liquidity providers and ballooning spreads may occur, but if so it is due to the nature of a free market and not the decision of the brokerage firm.

Market-maker FX firms are also accused of **stop harvesting** (or running stops), which is the practice of artificially spiking prices higher or lower to trigger the working stop-loss orders of clients. We discuss order types in detail later on, but as a primer, stop-loss orders are instructions to execute an order if the market moves adversely to a certain price. It is fair to say that if stop harvesting exists it is a substantial disadvantage to retail traders.

Stop harvesting is difficult to prove but is certainly a risk taken by any client who chooses to trade through a dealing-desk FX firm. To drive the point home at the risk of sounding repetitive, if the anxiety of stop harvesting will be lurking in the back of your mind, it doesn't matter whether or not the brokerage firm is engaged in stop running at all because you should be with a firm that offers access to an ECN. There are enough stressful scenarios and challenges in trading; the last thing you need to be doing is questioning whether or not market losses are due to poor trading decisions or an unethical market maker.

With that said, traders in *all arenas* tend to complain about the practice of stop running. In the stock and futures markets, many believe that the larger traders with deep pockets make a living fishing for stop orders. In my opinion, we are all best off accepting the fact that, regardless of the cause, stop orders have a propensity for getting filled at inopportune times and we should simply trade accordingly. I'd go as far as to suggest that the traditional use of stop orders might even be antagonistic to successful trading, but we cannot do that topic justice within the scope of this text.

The bottom line is that dealing-desk brokers stand to profit from the losses of clients, and this leaves the door open to temptations of dishonesty. In fact, because of the obvious conflict of interest, the practice of acting as a market maker to client transactions is strictly forbidden in the futures industry. FOREX traders must genuinely ask themselves whether they are comfortable with this type of relationship given that the CFTC and NFA have deemed this practice to be unacceptable in other trading arenas.

Carry or Roll Charges

During the week, currencies in the FOREX market trade 24 hours per day without interruption, but that doesn't mean there isn't a point in time at which one session is separated from the other. The end of the international trading day occurs at 5:00 p.m. EST. This is when your brokerage house will take a snapshot of the day's trades, your open positions, and your current account stats to be displayed on the daily statement. Additionally, it is the official end of the global FX session in which traders are subject to delivery of the underlying currency. Remember, FX contracts are agreements to make or take delivery of the currency within two days of the original execution.

Specifically, at 5:00 p.m. EST most brokerages consider positions left open beyond this time to be "held overnight" and are, therefore, subject to delivery. Most speculators have little interest in taking delivery of the currencies they are trading; instead, they simply want to speculate on price swings by purchasing and selling currency agreements in the FOREX market. To avoid delivery of the actual currency, FX positions must be rolled over.

If you have ever traded futures before, the term **rollover** probably isn't a foreign concept. The process of rolling over to avoid delivery of the underlying asset in FOREX is identical to the process in futures, but delivery in FX is much more frequent (that is, daily versus monthly or quarterly).

To futures traders, the word "rollover" describes the practice of transferring positions from a contract that is expiring soon into a futures contract with a distant expiration and delivery date. Specifically, speculators roll over their positions to avoid delivery of the underlying position while maintaining a speculative stance in the market, and they do so by simply liquidating holdings in the expiring contract month and reestablishing in a contract with a distant expiration. For instance, if a trader is long a June Euro futures contract that is going into expiration but would like to continue holding a bullish position, she could sell the June futures contract and buy the September; this is what is meant by rolling over. In FX, the idea is the same but the mechanics and logistics are a bit different.

For FOREX traders, a rollover is sometimes called a **swap** and is dubbed so because it is the action of a trader "swapping" the settlement date of a transaction with another settlement date (or, in other words, "rolling" the settlement date of a transaction forward). Because taking delivery of the currency is a rare event by speculators, most brokerage firms simply do this automatically for their clients.

Despite similarities, there is a component of FX and rolling over that doesn't exist in futures trading—an interest rate differential. Because currencies in FOREX are traded in pairs, there are two different currencies along with two different interest rates associated with each. All currencies have overnight interbank interest rates tied to them; this is also known as the **money market rate.** The difference between these rates is used to determine the rollover charge, also referred to as a **carry charge**.

The process of rolling over incurs either a cost or a credit to trading accounts; as always, it is the base currency that dominates the pair. Essentially, a trader will be paid interest for holding a long position if the *base currency* has a higher rate of interest than the *quote currency*. Conversely, if the *base currency's* interest rate is lower than the *quote currency's*, the trader long the pair will be charged. Another way to look at the same scenario is, if the interest rate on the

> The base currency is always dominant. It is the component of the pair that is bought and sold, and it is the element that determines whether the rollover process incurs a charge or triggers a credit.

currency you bought is higher than the rate of the currency you sold, you will earn "the roll." Like currency rates, interest rates fluctuate and, therefore, the carry or roll charges are not constant.

Rollover rates vary from brokerage to brokerage, so this might be something you want to consider when choosing a brokerage firm. Ultimately, the carry changes are based on interest rates that your brokerage firm has no control over, but banks tend to offer better rates to brokers with larger books of business. So, in theory, trading with a bigger FOREX firm might translate into favorable rollover rates.

If you will strictly be day trading, rollover rates should not be of any concern to you, but it is important that you understand the concept should you find yourself in a situation where you hold a position beyond 5:00 p.m. EST. That said, you should never limit your trading strategy to the 5:00 p.m. close simply to avoid the inconvenience of a roll charge. By doing this, you will be indirectly hindering your strategy from working in the manner it should (technical indicators aren't time based) and will likely pay more in transaction costs attempting to avoid a roll charge than the actual charge itself.

As you can see, currency traders are indirectly (or perhaps directly) speculating on interest rates. It is the FOREX rollover and carry charges that encourage the carry trade that is so often referred to on business news stations and FOREX blogs. Specifically, a **carry trade** is a strategy in which an investor trades a currency pair in a manner in which he is selling the currency with a relatively low rate of interest and buying the currency with a higher rate of interest. The goal of the trade is to benefit from the differential in interest rates, or simply earn more interest on the long currency than is being paid on the short currency.

Some carry trades have garnered "bandwagon followers" and have had dramatic impacts on currency valuation; one of the most compelling was the Yen carry trade that took place in the mid-to-late 2000s. Traders bought higher-interest-bearing currencies such as the U.S. Dollar and sold the Yen (which was backed by historically low rates near zero) looking to "earn carry." In such a trade, the assumption is that the currency exchange rate will remain relatively constant and the trader will earn the interest rate differential between the two currencies. The result was a historically cheap Yen, but when it came time for traders to unwind the over-popular carry trade, the Yen gained value in dramatic fashion as traders bought Yen and sold other currencies to offset positions. By the late 2000s, however, central banks around the world had lowered interest rates to record levels in an attempt to stabilize domestic economies, and this created a difficult environment for carry traders. Examples such as this are a glaring reminder that there simply isn't "easy" money to be made in any market…even when you have yields padding your risk and adding income to your position.

Tips and Tricks for Navigating FX Brokerage Firms

The work is not done after traders decide which FOREX brokerage type they are most comfortable with; there is an overwhelming number of factors to consider when choosing a specific brokerage to trust with your business. For instance, firms often offer traders incentives for being a client, demo accounts to show off their software, and various methods of account funding. Similarly, upon opening the account, a great amount of consideration should be given to the amount of money allocated to FX speculation and to the possibility of trading peripheral products, such as futures, within the same account. Here are a few guidelines intended to help weigh these choices.

FOREX Rebates

Some FX firms entice traders to open accounts by promising them cash back. Yes, that's right…cash back. The idea is that the brokerage firm, or an affiliate, agrees to give traders a rebate on each trade executed. This is similar to a commission charge, but in reverse; this time it is the client who receives the commission and the brokerage firm that pays it.

As appealing as this arrangement sounds, it is simply a clever marketing ploy to pad the profits of brokerage firms. This is true of nearly any instance in which buyers are lured into an arrangement via the promise of a rebate. For example, auto dealers commonly entice customers with the option of financing the purchase of a new car at a zero percent interest rate *or* taking a multi-thousand-dollar rebate. Clearly, if you are foregoing a large rebate to obtain an interest-free loan you are, in essence, paying all of the interest up front. On the other hand, if you opt for the rebate, you are receiving money from the get-go but will pay it back plus some in interest over the life of the loan, assuming you don't pay the balance off early. The point I am trying to stress is that rebates are intended to manipulate the behavior of consumers, but the rewards are often more smoke and mirrors than reality. Accordingly, brokerage rebates shouldn't be a deciding factor in choosing a brokerage firm. In fact, we'll look at some reasons why you should avoid firms that offer "cash-back" trading.

FX rebates vary from firm to firm, but are all based on the number of transactions executed. For instance, most firms that offer rebates pay their clients 1 to .5 pips for every round-turn trade. A **round turn** equates to both the purchase and sale of an equal quantity of a particular currency pair. Therefore, if a trader is promised a rebate of .5 pips buys 100,000 of the EUR/USD and later sells the 100,000 back, he is entitled to a rebate of $5. This is figured by taking the pip value of the EUR/USD and multiplying it by .5. As we learn in Chapter 5, "FOREX Trading Quotes and Calculations," if the U.S. Dollar is the quote currency of a pair, no conversions are necessary and a pip will *always* be equal to $10 per 100,000 units. It is easy to see how this might be appealing; a trader who buys and sells 500,000 worth of the EUR/USD in a trading session will "earn" $25!

Unfortunately, people tend to ignore the downside of a FOREX rebate arrangement…and there are several. For starters, if the firm responsible for handling your account can give you an attractive rebate simply for executing trades, it is reasonable to assume it is over-charging you in the first place. Rebates are typically offered by dealing-desk brokers, which means traders face fixed pip spreads, which frankly means wider pip spreads and higher transaction costs. For example, in the case of a dealing-desk broker that profits from the pip spread, if the spread provided to a client in the EUR/USD is 3 pips (or $30), even with a .5 pip rebate going back to the client, there is plenty of profit margin for those facilitating the transactions. An equally beneficial, or better, arrangement for the client would be tighter pip spreads; however, humans react to cash back more favorably than cash that was never missed, and this makes rebates a potent marketing tool.

In addition, FX rebates act is a powerful incentive to overtrade. It is easy to justify executing a trade if you know you will get $5 back every time you do it. Nonetheless, it is hardly a risk-free money printing press. The $5 rebate barely dents the true transaction cost of the trade—and even if it did, there is still market risk. The immediate purchase and sale of a currency pair will be a losing proposition due to the pip spread, but knowing most traders lose suggests the market risk associated with trading solely for the rebate is substantial.

Who Pays Rebates?

In most cases, FX cash rebates are actually paid by introducing brokers rather than the firm executing trades on behalf of clients via their dealing desk or an ECN. An **introducing broker** is a firm that solicits accounts for the FOREX dealer; you might also hear this entity referred to as an IB. In its simplest form, an IB is a broker, or group of brokers, that opens accounts on behalf of the FOREX dealer in exchange for an agreed-on commission to be paid by the dealer to the IB. It is similar to the arrangement that a typical broker would have working directly for the FX dealer, but instead of being paid as an employee (IRS forms W-2 and W-9) she is paid as a contractor (IRS form 1099).

Simply put, a FOREX dealer pays a volume-based commission to an introducing broker for the service of opening FX accounts and bringing clients to the firm. In turn, some introducing brokers pay their clients a rebate, in a lesser amount of the commission received from the FX dealer, as an incentive to choose their brokerage firm over others. From the introducing broker's viewpoint, the rebates make it easier to attract new clients and encourages them to trade; both of these ultimately result in more commission earned.

In most cases—and especially if you are trading with a U.S.-based brokerage firm—trading rebates are not deposited into the trader's FOREX account. Instead, they are distributed via methods such as PayPal, check, bank wire, and ACH electronic bank transfer.

Checking the NFA's BASIC System

The following description can be found on the NFA's website (www. nfa.futures.org):

> "The National Futures Association is the industry-wide, self-regulatory organization for the U.S. futures industry. The NFA

strives every day to safeguard market integrity, protect investors and help our members meet their regulatory responsibility."

In essence, the NFA is the governmental body in charge of enforcing commodity and, more recently, FX regulations set forth by the CFTC (Commodity Futures Trading Commission).

Perhaps one of the most beneficial services provided to traders by the NFA is the ability to access a database of current and past FX and futures brokerage firms. This database is known simply as BASIC (Background Affiliation Status Information Center) and is available on the home page of www.nfa.futures.org.

Within BASIC, it is possible to reveal the registration status and disciplinary history of the brokerage firm and individual broker you are dealing with, or are considering dealing with. Specifically, BASIC contains the length of your broker's time in the business as a registered member of the regulatory bodies and a list of any regulatory actions. Listed actions include NFA arbitration awards and CFTC reparation cases involving the broker; the same information can be found on the background of a brokerage firm.

It is important to realize that listed CFTC reparations do not imply guilt. A displayed claim may have been settled, dismissed, or withdrawn but will be on the BASIC record of the broker for as long as the database is available. As you can imagine, although the intention is to protect investors, false assumptions regarding the ethics of some industry insiders can sometimes be an unintended consequence.

I recommend that you confront your broker to discuss any possible infringements of regulations or ethics. After all, it is your money, and you deserve to fully understand the caliber of the person you will be hiring to help you find your way around the currency markets, regardless of whether you choose FX or futures.

The NFA's online BASIC database also provides traders with information on any NFA arbitrations. Unlike the previously discussed CFTC reparations, which involve a possible infraction of regulation, NFA arbitration is a dispute-resolution forum. Naturally, you would likely want to know whether your broker may have been party to questionable practices in the past. However, once again it is only fair that you get his side of the story because simply being part of an arbitration hearing may not translate into any wrongdoing.

FOREX Demo Account Dilemma

Trading technology paved the way for the explosion in foreign exchange speculation in the 2000s as firms began to offer electronic execution of currencies via "free" trading platforms. These platforms enabled clients to trade from home computers, laptops, and eventually smart phones. Word spread fast of commission-free, broker-free trading through one-click order entry platforms. However, what most retail traders didn't realize was that demo accounts were sometimes used as sales ploys to get traders excited about the possibilities of abnormal profits.

Not only do demo accounts lure in traders with flashing lights, point-and-click trade capabilities, and plenty of excitement, they also give FX brokers the ability to skew demo account results. I am not suggesting that all FX brokers do this, but it is a practice that many have been accused of and you should be aware of the possibility. Just as dealing desks are rumored to spike prices to run stop orders to the disadvantage of live trading accounts, they have been said to do the opposite in client demo accounts. For instance, a demo trade might avoid a stop order being triggered in the same environment in which a live account would have. As you can imagine, this could favorably skew the profits in a demo account and therefore give the soon-to-be client a misconception of the realities involved. Naturally, the demo trader builds up a false sense of confidence only to find that once real money is on the line, his stop order "always" seems to get triggered at the worst possible time. Similarly, it feels as though the otherwise well-timed profit-taking orders to get filled less frequently in a live account than was the case with the demo.

To be fair, the phenomenon of gangbuster profits in demo trading, followed by account draining losses in live trading, isn't new. Although there is less skepticism of broker practices relating to stock or futures demo accounts, demo traders tend to have similar experiences in these arenas. After all, it is much easier to make money in demonstration trading that it is in a live trading account. There are a few explanations for this, but the most significant is that when your hard-earned cash is on the line, emotions of fear, greed, and frustration often take hold. Although making "Monopoly" money in a demo account is fun and exciting, losing it doesn't inflict much pain on the trader. However, even a small amount of actual money lost is like a dagger to the heart. Unfortunately, the psychological effects are sometimes too much to take for an inexperienced trader.

In other words, if you have been a successful paper trader or have made boat loads of money in a demo account, congratulations—but don't expect the same amount of success in a live account. In my opinion, trading is only 20% strategy and execution; the other 80% is mental. In a demo account, traders are only able to test 20% of what will eventually determine whether they will be profitable in their venture.

Funding a FOREX Account

The funding of a stock, bond, and futures trading account is typically limited to traditional methods such as a personal check, bank wire, or ETF (electronic fund transfer). In some instances, brokerage firms will accept certified checks or bank drafts, but due to strict anti-money-laundering rules, it is best to adhere to the first three means. Also, some brokerage firms will hold checks for a specified number of days to ensure the client has funds available in the account the check is being drafted upon, or even until it officially clears, which could take up to ten days. That said, most futures brokerage firms will treat checks the "same as cash" for clients who have displayed an adequate financial background and integrity.

Because futures are leveraged, commodity brokerage firms are taking on a considerable amount of risk to allow clients to trade accounts funded by checks. Should it be discovered that a client check bounces due to insufficient funds or an account freeze, it is the brokerage firm that is responsible for ensuring funding is available to cover any trading losses until the client is able to correct the situation. Given the leverage provided by the markets, it is possible that a considerable amount of damage could be done prior to the discovery of insufficient funds. Naturally, this leaves a broker in the hole for the amount of the losses realized on trades margined by funds that never really existed in the first place. This protocol is necessary to enabling the exchange to guarantee each market transaction because without holding the brokerage liable, the exchange would either have to "eat" the difference or introduce traders to counter-party risk in trading execution. I hate to admit it, but I am speaking from a painfully expensive experience. Unfortunately, futures and FOREX brokers have many of the same credit risks traditional lenders and credit card issuers face.

Because the FX industry was born in an environment lacking regulation, the methods in which a trading account can be funded are much more creative than that of the aforementioned conventional methods. Although the U.S. government, namely the NFA and CFTC, has begun regulating FOREX, it was nearly impossible for it to step in after the fact and completely revamp the way business had been conducted for years.

The goal of FOREX brokers is to open accounts and get them trading as soon as possible; after all, they make a living off of transaction fees, and the quicker a client begins to trade, the faster the revenue stream begins. Accordingly, to facilitate the speed of getting an account up and running, many FX firms have opted to accept untraditional forms of account funding, such as credit cards, debit cards, and even online money transfer services such as PayPal and Moneybookers. In fact, these methods are encouraged because the funds are nearly instant, guaranteed to be valid upon arrival, enable the client to avoid the wait time associated with writing a check, and bypass the bank fees of a wire transfer.

> It is better to be out of the market wishing you were in, than in the market wishing you were out.

Credit card funding is the fastest and cheapest way to fund a FOREX account; in almost all instances, the funds will post to your trading account immediately. Nonetheless, not all FX firms accept credit card funding. For instance, many of the futures brokerage firms that offer FX as a side product to their primary business, do not allow clients to fund via credit card. This might partly be due to a moral obligation they feel to the industry given that accepting credit card funding for futures accounts is illegal, but it is likely due to the compliance nightmare that could arise from such drastically different practices under the same roof.

What is best for the welfare of the broker isn't always best for the client; as appealing as credit card funding might sound, it is not a recommended method. This is because funding with credit entails magnifying leverage in the already fast-moving currency markets. In other words, not only are traders enjoying 50-to-1 leverage (or higher for non-U.S. clients) but those funding with a credit card are using borrowed funds to meet the margin requirement! In essence, instead of putting down $2,000 to margin a $100,000 FX contract, the trader isn't putting anything down other than his credit card and an obligation to pay the creditor back at a later date. It is easy to see how such a practice could lead to trouble. Even those who are diligent in paying off their credit card balance at the end of every month will be tempted to use more credit to refund their trading accounts in an attempt to recover market losses. It wouldn't take much to reach the point where it is impossible for them to pay it back without incurring months or years of interest charges from their creditor bank. Simply put, using a credit card to fund a trading account is an unnecessary enticement to use too much leverage. Also, the convenience and speed of credit card funding will likely magnify the temptations of refunding accounts at a time when the trader's mental state isn't ideal for FOREX trading.

How Much Should Traders Fund Their Accounts With?

The bottom line is the only person who can answer this question is the trader himself. However, I can give you guidelines to funding a speculative currency account, regardless of whether you opt for futures or FX.

Although traders can't control the amount of margin required to hold any given position, they *can* control the leverage they trade with. Obviously more funding in the account per unit traded equates to lighter leverage. In turn, the risk and emotional hardship will be more tolerable. Unfortunately, most traders have a tendency to be satisfied with meeting the minimum margin requirements and thus expose their egos, and their trading accounts, to a significant amount of volatility.

As a rule of thumb, I recommend traders deposit *at least* four times the amount required to trade any given currency pair. Therefore, if the margin required to hold 100,000 units of the EUR/USD in an FX account is $2,800, it's probably a good idea to have somewhere around $10,000 or more. Once again, the premise of doing this is to reduce leverage, so depositing $10,000 while simultaneously increasing the trading size to 300,000 does nothing in regard to taming risk, or promoting reward. Similarly, using the same leverage ratio, a trader could theoretically hold 10,000 units in an account for as little as $280 but should have at least $1,000 on deposit.

> When it comes to leverage, sometimes *less* is actually *more!*

Over-funding a trading account will cut down on the adrenaline rush, but it might also prevent the inevitable "rush" to account-depleting trading, and I see this as a positive trade-off. More margin and less leverage immediately provides traders with more room for error, and simultaneously shifts the odds of success in the desired direction.

NFA's No-Hedging Rules

One of the biggest bombshells dropped on the FOREX industry by the NFA following their "intrusion" into the currency markets was Compliance Rule 2-43. The rule prohibits FX traders from using a technique known as **hedging.** In FOREX, the term hedging is used to describe a practice that is a little different from what one might infer from the traditional meaning of the term. In its conventional form, hedging is a method whereby traders attempt to reduce risk exposure in any particular market or even an entire portfolio. In general, hedging takes on many forms, including the purchase of options to ensure against adverse price movements, or buying and selling related financial instruments with the idea that doing so will reduce the volatility of current holdings.

> Hedging in FOREX isn't "hedging" at all; it is completely eliminating market risk on all "hedged" contracts rather than simply mitigating it. With risk elimination also comes the elimination of profit potential.

However, when FX traders refer to hedging, they are speaking of a very specific strategy in which traders are *both long* and *short* the same pair within the same trading account. To recap, the strategy of FX hedging isn't to buy or sell a *related* instrument to reduce risk, it is to buy or sell the *same* instrument to completely *eliminate* (not mitigate) the risk.

This version of hedging is not possible in stocks and futures; in those markets a trader can be either long or short but cannot be both long *and* short the same instrument at the same time. In the futures market, if a trader is short a contract and then buys the same contract, he is simply flat the market or no longer has an open position. This is also true of stocks. However, in FX, traders were originally allowed to instruct their trading platform either to open a new

Remember, traders who buy a currency pair are said to be "long" and those who sell are "short." FX hedgers are both long and short the same instrument simultaneously.

position or to offset an existing position. If the latter option was the case, they could be long and short the same market at the same time. Again, among FOREX traders this is known as hedging and is no longer possible for U.S. clients due to NFA Compliance Rule 2-43.

Regulators have good arguments against this type of hedging. For one, despite what you might read on the Internet, there isn't a mathematical benefit from being long and short the same instrument at the same time. For every pip the market moves up or down, the trader will be making a pip on one side and losing a pip on the other. This is true regardless of how fast or far the market moves.

Some FX traders who have employed a hedging strategy believe being long and short at the same time enables them to lock in a profit on one side of the trade, with hopes of doing the same on the other side should the market retrace. Nonetheless, the trader isn't any better off doing this as he would be waiting for the market to make its move in one direction and then taking a position on the opposite side.

Let's take a look at an example: A trader who is long 100,000 GBP/USD from 1.6571 and later sells 100,000 at 1.6571 to open a short position has locked in a break-even proposition on the trade but is now simultaneously long and short the same pair. Ignoring implications of the bid and ask spread, if the price of the British Pound versus the U.S. Dollar increases by 100 pips to 1.6671, the trader is losing 100 pips on the 100,000 short pair and making 100 pips on the long position. Clearly the trader is still breaking even on the trade. If the long position is offset at 1.6671 at a profit of 100 pips, the cash proceeds are credited to the trading account but the liability of the 100 pip loss offsets any benefit.

However, once locking in a profit on the long pair, the trader stands to reduce the loss on the short pair should the market retrace some of the gains. Any reduction in loss in this pair translates into an overall profit on the trade because the trader is no longer losing as much as was gained on the long position. Assuming the price of the GBP/USD drops to 1.6621 and the trader is able to offset the short pair at this price, the loss on the short pair is only 50 pips while the profit on the long pair is 100. Accordingly, this trader would have made 50 pips on the trade using this "hedging strategy."

However, it is important to realize that this trader would have been just as well off not using the hedging strategy and simply executing a short position on the GBP/USD at a price of 1.6671 and buying it back at 1.6621. In fact, the second strategy would yield a higher return to the trader because of lower transaction costs. Whether this trade was done with an ECN broker charging an outright commission or by a dealing desk charging a pip spread for each pair executed, the transaction costs in the hedging scenario would "eat" more of the profit. Simply put, having no position at all is equivalent to being both long and short the same pair, in the same quantity, simultaneously, and saves the trader unnecessary transaction fees.

The NFA recognizes that the so-called hedging strategy offered no real benefit to the trader, but is a way for FOREX brokers to increase trading volume, and thus revenue. Their answer was the implementation of controversial Compliance Rule 2-43 prohibiting FOREX brokers from allowing hedging strategies. The rule was intended to save traders from themselves, but regardless of the good intentions, the FX community (both brokers and traders alike) generally disapprove of the regulation.

You may also hear Compliance Rule 2-43 referred to as the NFA's FIFO (First In First Out) rule. According to the rule, FX brokers must offset customer positions on a first-in, first-out basis. By nature of FIFO, customers are unable to carry both long and short positions. Nevertheless, the NFA did add a provision that enables the FOREX broker to, at the client's request, "offset the same-size transactions even if there are older transactions of a difference size." However, the regulation also stipulates that in such a case it must "offset the transaction against the oldest transaction of that size." Plainly, a trader who is trading both mini and standard-sized FX contracts can offset mini positions first even if they are newer, or vice versa.

Trading FX and Futures, Side by Side

Because of similarities between the futures and FOREX trading communities, it should come as no surprise that many futures brokerage firms offer FX trading to their clients. After all, FX is seen as a significant threat to the market share of futures speculators, and early on when marketing tactics went unregulated this phenomenon was magnified. On the other hand, brokerage firms that opened their doors specifically to provide traders access to the world of FX typically don't offer futures trading to their clients. There are several reasons for this, but it's largely due to the additional regulation and clearing arrangements required to provide futures brokerage services. In other words, FX is the "laundromat" of the financial industry in that it is considered to be one of the easiest formats in regard to "startup" firms. However, this is quickly changing as the NFA and CFTC gain more ground on regulation. In fact, the pendulum is even starting to swing the other way. Massive capital requirements required by regulators of U.S. FX brokers have essentially forced many firms out of the business. Some were deserving due to questionable practices and others were innocent victims of a changing industry.

Don't forget, because FX is not traded on a centralized exchange, dealing-desk FX brokers are accustomed to executing and clearing trades in a synthetic market that they have created solely for their clients. With these dealing-desk FX brokers calling the shots for so long, it is easy to see why they would be reluctant to offer exchange traded services in which they have much less control over the situation.

Also, a handful of stock trading firms have added futures and FX trading "on the side" as a means of preventing capital from leaving their brokerage firms and going to those that offer alternative markets. Nonetheless, it is important to realize that such firms are merely attempting to *meet* the needs of traders but typically aren't capable of offering superior services. In many cases, they have little support for leveraged products and offer a limited number of them anyway. You probably wouldn't order spaghetti at a Chinese restaurant, so why would you trade derivatives with a stock broker?

In any case, brokers that offer futures and FX trading within the same platform are actually maintaining two separate client accounts: one for each asset class. This makes sense given that FX and futures are two completely separate trading arenas and must follow rules and regulations exclusive to the respective industry. Accordingly, despite the fact that you will be able to see your positions on the same screen and with a single account balance, you will likely receive two different statements with two different account numbers. Some brokers offer what are called **combined statements,** which are statements that combine the total cash and positions in multiple accounts, such as a futures account and an FX account, within a single statement. This doesn't mean that it is a single account; it is simply a convenience offered by the brokerage firm to mitigate confusion.

Trading futures or FX with a stock broker is like ordering an Italian dish from a Chinese restaurant—it will probably look the same, but the smell and taste will likely fall short of expectations.

4

Is FOREX the Currency Casino?

W hether you are trading stocks, bonds, futures, or FX, one thing remains constant: the market will be what you want it to be. For instance, if you are trading for the adrenaline rush, there are certainly plenty of opportunities to abuse leverage and place speculative bets with large potential rewards but equivalently dismal odds. On the other hand, if you are the type of trader who is simply looking for a speculative vehicle to take calculated risks accompanied with positive odds of success, the markets can be that too.

In the spring of 2011, the FX markets had already experienced a decade of exponential growth followed by a few years of U.S. regulatory bodies pulling in the reins on the industry. In April of 2011, *Barron's* published an article depicting the big picture of FOREX, and the inferences weren't all positive. According to *Barron's,* FX brokers face a much higher attrition rate than stock brokers, with 15% to 20% of accounts closing per year as opposed to 5% in equities.

> "Survive first, and make money afterwards."
> —George Soros

To be frank, I was surprised it was that low. As poor of a stat as that is, it seems to be a positive given the assumption that approximately 75% of FX traders lose money. Despite consistent volume growth in FX, many are wondering whether continued expansion is possible considering of the extent of investors' losses. Along with word spreading about the difficulties of profitable trading in FOREX, a new CFTC rule

> "If you personalize losses, you can't trade."
> —Bruce Kovner

requires that FX brokers disclose to potential clients the percentage of accounts held by the firm that have been profitable in previous quarters. For instance, one of the largest FX brokers, Gain Capital (also operating as FOREX.com), was required to admit that in the third quarter of 2010 77% of their client accounts were producing negative results and approximately 72% were in the red at the end of the fourth quarter. To make things worse, 37% of Gain Capital clients funded their accounts in 2010 with credit cards and therefore could be paying high rates of interest on money that was quickly lost in the currency markets. Perhaps more realistic given the recent tendency for credit card borrowers to default, many banks were left with large unpaid balances racked up by irresponsible FX traders.

The same brokerage revealed that although the average account size is just $3,000, the firm generates nearly as much in transaction costs per year on a similar sized account. This painfully illustrates that despite being hidden, transaction costs certainly add up quickly.

The purpose of mentioning the dark side of FOREX probabilities isn't to scare you away, or to shed a negative light on FX brokers (especially Gain Capital). The goal is to give you a realistic idea of what to expect in order to avoid becoming a statistic. The truth is, speculating in *any* market comes with unfavorable odds. By nature, a speculator is attempting to beat the market and doing so requires having some sort of edge over all other participants; trading successfully isn't impossible, but it isn't easy either.

> Trading on leverage is a form of gambling, but it is up to the trader to determine the game and the odds by adjusting leverage and paying attention to probabilities of success.

In fact, I would venture to say that those who are attempting to day-trade equities or are using leverage in their stock "investments" probably face similarly challenged probabilities. As a derivatives broker, I've come to realize that the winners-to-losers ratio is probably somewhere near 20/80. Therefore, although only FX brokers are required to provide prospective clients with win/loss stats, that doesn't mean other venues will provide any better odds.

Who Is to Blame for Excessive Losses in FX by Retail Traders?

Now that we have established the fact that most leveraged speculators walk away from the markets with less than they started with, let's discuss where the fault might lie. It is convenient to blame the brokerage firms, but in my view the probability of success, along with the magnitude of profits and losses, is only partially the result of the chosen venue (although it does matter). The rest lies in how the trader places his bets and manages his chips.

Without a doubt, leverage is one of the features of FX and futures that attracts retail speculators and gives them the opportunity to earn abnormal profits, but what some fail to acknowledge is that leverage is also the primary contributor to vast losses across speculative currency accounts. The more leverage used, the less room for error—and the more likely losses will pile up. In other words, leverage is a double-edged sword, and it's probably better to work toward converting it into a butter knife.

For example, as we now know, U.S. FOREX traders are granted 50-to-1 leverage, but they can increase their odds of success substantially by simply choosing to use less leverage. As a reminder, a trader might be required to hold $2,000 in a trading account to purchase $100,000 in nominal value of a currency, but she can reduce the leverage used to 25 to 1 by funding the account with $4,000 or to 12.5 to 1 by funding with $8,000, and so on.

Not only do currency traders have a tendency to over-leverage themselves, but they are also inclined to over-trade. Rather than wait for what are deemed to be high probability entries, a lack of patience often lures traders into markets prematurely out of boredom. This lack of discipline is often too much for a speculative account to take and can easily lead to a depletion of funds.

In reality, currencies are far less volatile than equities on a percentage basis, but because of the leverage granted to traders in both the FX and futures markets, they have garnered a bad reputation. Nonetheless, I think it is fair to say

> "Never invest in any idea you can't illustrate with a crayon."
> —Peter Lynch

that, similar to the mantra "guns don't kill people, people kill people," "currency markets don't bankrupt trading accounts, people bankrupt trading accounts."

Self-Directed FOREX

Because FOREX wasn't available to retail speculators until after the technology and Internet boom, and because the industry was built on the concept of so-called commission-free trading, FX accounts are primarily self-directed. In other words, FOREX brokerage firms typically expect their clients to enter trades via an online trading platform with little assistance from a professional broker. For those who aren't comfortable placing FX trades online, most brokers provide a 24-hour trade desk— but don't expect to get any opinions, guidance, or education when you call. They are there to place trades at your discretion and are generally not licensed or educated on the details; therefore, they shouldn't be considered a source of reliable information or opinion. In general, dealing-desk brokerage firms, or those strictly offering FX trading, tend not to offer full-service accounts.

On the other hand, you can find some full-service FX brokers out there, but they are few and far between. Conversely, many of the full-service futures brokerage firms that offer FX as a side product frequently have several individual brokers who are capable of meeting the needs of both futures and FX traders who are looking for a little hand-holding.

I happen to be one of those brokers who offers currency trading in both venues. Accordingly, although many of our clients are self-directed in futures and FOREX, we are equipped to offer full service, regardless of the market they choose. Because of this, I likely have a biased opinion in regard to the use of full-service brokers, but I feel I would be short-changing you if I didn't mention some of my observations.

Throughout my career, I have witnessed massive leaps in technology provided to traders, with far more market transparency and access than was once the case. Once upon a time, placing trades was something that could only be done by picking up the phone, but in today's world orders might be submitted to a full-service broker by e-mail, instant message, or text message. Further, those comfortable with their knowledge of the market and their computer skills can easily buy and sell hundreds of thousands of dollars worth of currency with a single click of the mouse.

In addition to market access, traders now have the ability to analyze markets in a way that simply wasn't available to traders in the 1990s. Charting has gone from something done with paper and pencil, to the realm of complex computer software that charts pricing in real time and enables users to electronically analyze price movement—they can even let a pre-programmed algorithm tell them when to buy or sell.

Ironically, none of these advances in technology seem to have increased the odds of success. Although it would be hard to prove mathematically, it appears the win-loss percentages for retail traders have remained constant.

Perhaps all the conveniences of modern technology breed bad habits such as over-active trading, taking on too much leverage, and simply being unprepared for the task at hand. After all, with the barriers to entry so low, it is quite possible (and in my opinion probable) that many of today's online traders are truly not educated to the realities of leveraged speculation. Nonetheless, the appeal of "saving" money on commission seems to be greater than the fear of unnecessary losses in the markets due to a lack of experience. Trust me, rookie mistakes in judgment and placing trades can far outweigh the cost of paying commission to a broker that might be effective in shortening the learning curve.

Trading Crude Oil, Gold, and Silver in FX Accounts

In an effort to acquire clients from existing futures firms, newly budding FOREX firms have opted to offer trading in spot commodities such as crude oil, gold, and silver. The marketing premise was to lure futures traders with the appeal of so-called commission-free trading and lower margin rates than what was offered on regulated exchange-traded futures.

Spot gold trading in FX is done via the XAU/USD pair, or Gold versus U.S. Dollar, and just like any other currency pair, the trader is buying or selling gold (the base currency) against the greenback. In other words, buying the XAU/USD pair means the trader is going long gold and simultaneously selling the Dollar. The price of the pair reflects the value of the metal in terms of the U.S. Dollar. Thus, if XAU/USD is bid at 1508.45 with an ask of 1509.05, a trader buying the pair at the market would pay $1509.05. In the case of silver, the pair traded would be XAG/USD.

The XAU/USD pair represents the price of 1 troy ounce of gold; as the value of gold increases relative to the U.S. Dollar, the price of the pair appreciates to reflect the increase in valuation of the metal and the decrease in the Dollar. On the other hand, if the price of gold decreases, it will take fewer U.S. Dollars to purchase a troy ounce of gold, and therefore the price of the pair will decline.

> "Wall Street people learn nothing and forget everything."
> —Peter Lynch

Although the quote of the XAU/USD represents 1 troy ounce, the contract size is actually 10 ounces. Accordingly, for each pip of price movement, which is equivalent to a penny in regard to the actual value of gold, the trader actually stands to make or lose a dime ($0.01 × 10 = $0.10). It doesn't sound like much, but as with any leveraged product it adds up quickly and many traders have a tendency to unwisely take advantage of the massive leverage provided. Nonetheless, if trading one lot (10 ounces of gold) of the XAU/USD pair, a trader long from 1508.80 who sells at 1510.80 will have made $20—that is, (1510.80 − 1508.80) × 10 ounces = $20. Had the same trader executed two contracts (20 ounces), the profit would have been $40, and had the trader executed ten contracts (100 ounces), he would have made $200.

In relation to profit, loss, and size, trading ten FX lots of the XAU/USD pair is identical to trading one lot of the traditional gold futures contract listed on the COMEX exchange operated by the CME Group. Similar to ten XAU/USDs, a gold futures contract represents 100 troy ounces and exposes traders to $100 in profit or loss per $1 price change in gold.

In regard to positions held "overnight," as defined by having an open position beyond the close of the official day session, FOREX brokers offer much more leverage in metals trading than futures brokers. Nevertheless, because futures brokers offer day traders discounted margin rates, the intraday leverage between futures and FX is comparable. In fact, some futures brokers might even enable traders to use much more leverage than FX traders enjoy. We'll discuss futures day trading margin in detail in the next section.

In my opinion, there are glaring arguments for trading metals futures as opposed to their spot market counterparts. For starters, the bid and ask spread on a spot gold pair is typically 50 to 70 pips, and this equates to $5 to $6 per lot! A trader who has executed ten contracts to reach the contract size of the CME Group's gold futures contract would pay about $55 in hidden transaction costs via the difference between the bid and the ask. In comparison, even *full-service* futures brokers tend to charge far less than that, and *online futures* traders are typically trading at a fraction of the cost. Unsurprisingly, futures traders also face the obstacle of a naturally occurring bid/ask spread, but it is generally much smaller than that of FOREX. The typical spread in gold futures is a mere .10 to .20 in price, or the equivalent of $10 to $20 to a futures trader, which is far less than the $50 to $60 faced by spot gold traders.

Additionally, CME Group metals futures are exchange traded, highly regulated, and vastly liquid. FX metals, on the other hand, are typically offered only by dealing desks in which clients are trading against the very firm they are trusting to provide them with reliable market access and execution.

As this book was going to print, new U.S. regulations were in the process of being debated, and possibly implemented, that would essentially prevent U.S. FOREX brokers from offering access to off-exchange spot metals and crude oil trading. Nonetheless, traders can feel comfortable and confident CME metals futures are here to stay.

FX Leverage Versus Futures Leverage

We have already discussed the fact that FOREX leverage is variable, whereas futures margin is relatively constant. Although futures exchanges have the ability to adjust margin requirements at any time, they rarely do so. In the event exchanges opt to make margin requirement changes, they are often in effect for long periods of time before the next alteration. However, there are a few dynamics of margining in each arena that traders must be aware of.

The FOREX industry was built on the premise of undercutting the futures industry in regard to margin requirements. In the "early days" of FX trading, U.S. traders were offered leverage ratios well in excess of 100 to 1, and in some cases as much as 400 to 1. Obviously, this amount of leverage is great for the brokerage firm in that it encourages higher trading volume; however, if used, it provides the public with dismal odds of success.

> I compare aggressive marketing of ultra-low margin to selling glass candy to a baby. It is easy to do, but is the type of thing that should make it hard to sleep at night.

A typical currency futures contract carries a leverage ratio of about 50 to 1, identical to the maximum amount allowed by FX firms according to NFA regulations. However, futures brokers have the ability to provide day traders with discounted margin rates. Such rates are available to anybody who exits his position by the close of the designated day session. With this comes lower margin requirements and higher leverage in the futures markets relative to FX for intraday trades, despite the fact that FOREX traders face lower margin requirements for positions held "overnight." I certainly don't advocate using this type of leverage for strategies other than perhaps scalping, but it is nice to know that it is there for those who need it.

On another note, when it comes to choosing a trading arena, your decision shouldn't be based on which market will provide the most leverage. After all, that is similar to choosing an item on a fast food menu with the most fat. It has the potential to provide immediate gratification, but the end result is rarely a positive one.

5

FOREX Trading Quotes and
Calculations

P erhaps the biggest challenge faced by FOREX traders, aside from accurate price speculation, of course, is getting comfortable with the way FX pairs are quoted and calculated. Similar to the fractions that keep the math involved in commodity trading complex, FOREX traders must be at ease working in decimals. The goal of this chapter is to simplify the concept in an attempt to shorten the learning curve.

How FX Pairs Are Quoted

As we have discussed, all tradable markets have a bid and ask spread. This is true of baseball cards, houses, and even goods traded in pawn shops, but in the financial markets it is much more obvious. This is particularly true in FX because the bid and ask are blatantly highlighted. In fact, FOREX platforms provide traders with two prices for each currency pair, rather than a single quote; these two prices are the bid and the ask. To illustrate, in an FX platform, you might see the last price for the USD/CAD at 0.9553. This represents the most recent trade executed in the pair, but it doesn't tell the whole story. Yet, as we know, all FX platforms distinctly differentiate the price at which a pair can be bought or sold. In this example, you might see an ask quote of 0.9556 and a bid price of 0.9553; a trader going long the USD/CAD at the market price would pay 0.9556, and a trader selling at the market price would be filled at 0.9553, assuming there wasn't a requote due to fast market conditions. The difference between these prices is typically referred to as a *pip spread* in the world of FOREX. This term stems from the fact that the smallest increment of price movement in an FX pair is referred to as a *pip*.

Several futures and FX books are available that define the bid and ask from the market maker's perspective. However, I feel that doing so is an injustice to the average retail trader; more often than not it creates confusion rather than clarity. Therefore, for the majority of readers the "ask" will always represent the price to buy and the "bid" the price to sell. Clearly, this results in an immediate disadvantage because a trader who simultaneously buys and sells any given pair would sustain a loss in the amount of the pip spread. Accordingly, it is important to trade with a brokerage firm that offers competitive pip spreads; this typically implies a non-dealing desk broker with several liquidity providers within its offered ECN. ECN brokers often offer spreads of a pip or less!

FOREX Pricing

We have already determined that currency pairs are quoted to traders in bids and asks with the difference between the two prices being the pip spread. We also know that a pip in FOREX is equivalent to a tick in futures. In *most* cases, a pip is 1/10,000 or 0.0001 of a five-digit price quote; there are typically four digits to the right of the decimal and one to the left. Yet, in recent years, some brokerage firms and thus execution platforms have begun offering trading in fractions of a pip. In other words, a pip might not always be the smallest increment of price movement like it once was; it might be possible to trade a 1/2 or 1/10th of a pip, depending on the brokerage firm you use. Obviously, this complicates the definition of a pip, but as you begin dealing with the figures in more detail, the concept will become more clear. Let me try to simplify the notion before you close the book and give up on FX forever.

> Some brokers offer trading in fractions of a pip. If so, you might see six-digit quotes (rather than the usual five digits). Here are two EUR/USD examples:
>
> 1.22221 = $1.2222 and 1/10th of a pip
> 1.22225 = $1.2222 and 1/2 of a pip

Ignoring the possibility of trading in fractions of a pip, you might see the ask price of the GBP/USD pair at 1.5812, where the last digit in the quote represents the pip. If the ask price moves higher to 1.5814, a trader long the pair has profited by 2 pips and a trader short the pair has lost 2 pips. Remember, buying the GBP/USD equates to buying the British Pound and simultaneously selling the U.S. Dollar. In this example, if the Pound strengthened against the Dollar by 2 pips, or 0.0002, the trader who is long is profitable by 2 pips. Later we will determine how much money 2 pips really means to a trader.

Another way to look at this is that given the price change, it takes two 100ths of a cent more to purchase a single British Pound than was previously the case. It doesn't sound like much because without leverage, it isn't. However, with the leverage provided to traders in the FX markets, it is possible to make or lose substantial amounts of money on what are normally miniscule price changes.

I stated that most currencies are priced in five-digit quotes, but the exception to this format is the Yen, which consists of only four digits. Also differing from the majority of other currencies, for which there are four digits to the right of the decimal, the Yen is quoted with two digits to the left and two digits to the right of the decimal.

You might see the last trade in the USD/JPY at 84.10. In this instance, a 1-pip increase would result in a price of 84.11. However, it is possible for the USD/JPY to trade at a price above 100 (101.01 or higher), and in such a case the Yen will be quoted in five digits; however, there will always be only two digits on the right of the decimal. This is because, unlike the other currencies, which are inclined to be nearly equal to the U.S. dollar and see fluctuations above and below par (a one-to-one relationship), the Yen tends to hover near a 100-to-1 rate with the U.S. Dollar. In other words, the value of 1 Yen is closer to that of a penny than it is a Dollar; accordingly, it takes more Yen to buy a Dollar than it does a currency such as the Euro or the Canadian Dollar.

The True Value of a Pip

Unfortunately, there isn't a standardized or fixed value of a pip in FX as there is the tick in currency futures trading. In FOREX, the value of a pip is stated in terms of the quote currency and, therefore, its value will depend on the currency pair traded. However, for those currencies in which the U.S. Dollar is the quote currency, such as the EUR/USD,

GBP/USD, AUD/USD, and NZD/USD, a single pip will *always* be $10. This makes sense because a pip is 0.0001 of 100,000 (0.0001 × 100,000 = $10) on a standard lot. Similarly, a pip would equal $1 for a mini contract (0.0001 × 10,000) and 10 cents for a micro (0.0001 × 1,000). Calculating the value of a pip for currency pairs in which the USD is *not* the quote currency can be a little more difficult. This is because the pip value is in terms of another currency and must be converted into U.S. Dollars.

Traders could avoid the hassle of figuring pip values by strictly trading currencies in which the U.S. Dollar is the quote currency, but that probably isn't in their best interest. Believe it or not, many beginning FX traders either adopt such a practice or they simply trade other pairs without an understanding of the true risks and rewards, leaving the calculating up to their brokerage statement. Clearly, before traders put their hard-earned money on the line, they owe it to themselves to know the products they are trading and how much is at stake.

Let's take a look at an example in which it is necessary to convert the profit and loss pips into U.S. Dollars. A trader buying or selling the USD/CHF will make or lose 10 (0.0001 × 100,000) Swiss Francs on a standard lot trade for every pip the price moves up or down. To determine the true value to the trader, the 10 Francs must be converted to the native currency, which in this case is the U.S. Dollar.

If the USD/CHF is trading at 0.9521, it costs 0.9521 Francs to buy 1 U.S. Dollar. Knowing this, we can determine the pip value to the trader is equal to about $10.50. This can be figured by dividing 0.0001 (1 pip) by the going Franc rate of 0.9521 and multiplying by the contract size (100,000 for a standard lot). Naturally, if each pip is worth about $10.50 to a trader, 10 pips is equal to $105.00 (10 × 10.50).

1 Swiss Franc pip = (0.0001/0.9521) × 100,000 = $10.50

If the trader were executing orders in mini contracts, rather than full-sized contracts, the pip value would be less. Given the same exchange rate, a mini FX trader would make or lose about $1.05 per pip of price movement—that is, (0.0001/0.9521) × 10,000. Accordingly, 10 pips in a mini lot is equal to about $10.50.

One of the biggest turnoffs to trading currencies in the FX market is the hassle of converting profits and losses back to U.S. Dollars, or whichever your domestic currency might be. However, if looked at methodically, the process is much more overwhelming in concept than it is in practice. Luckily, however, FX trading platforms are capable of doing the math for you. Also, several online FX calculators are provided by FOREX educators and news services. One example is www.BabyPips.com. Traders simply input the pertinent information and click a button. Even so, it is a good idea for you to understand the process simply so you will be aware of your risk and reward potential prior to entering a trade— and on the off-chance that your brokerage firm is miscalculating, you will be knowledgeable enough to know something is amiss.

Keep in mind, in the U.S. most FX brokers display client balances in U.S. Dollars each day. In other words, statements are shown in terms of U.S. Dollars calculated at the exchange rate available at the New York FX market close at 5:00 p.m. EST. Therefore, even trades executed in currency pairs that have quote currencies other than the USD will exhibit profit and loss in terms of the greenback. Simply put, just because you are trading pairs for which you are making or losing pips in the Euro, Pound, or any other currency, doesn't mean you will end up with a trading account full of an array of currencies.

6

What Are Currency Futures?

The futures markets, and the easy access to currency speculation they provide, have been in existence for decades. Therefore, in this book I've opted to put a little more focus into the relatively new, and somewhat unknown, world of FOREX. Nonetheless, it is critical that traders fully understand the opportunities available to them in the currency futures markets. In fact, as you will discover in reading this text, I tend to be an advocate of foreign exchange speculation through the centralized and regulated futures exchanges, as opposed to off-exchange products with little regulation (FOREX). If you are interested in learning about futures trading in detail, you might be interested in my book *A Trader's First Book on Commodities,* published by FT Press.

> "You could come in and get rich overnight, or you could lose, but there was opportunity," said Rick Santelli, a CNBC Business News commentator and veteran futures trader in reference to floor traders at the Chicago Mercantile Exchange. He added, "It's a bittersweet story." (From the movie *Floored.*)

Despite the futures market being the more mature marketplace, many beginning retail traders aren't aware of the ability to speculate in currencies via futures contracts—even worse, they aren't privy to the advantages of doing so. This is probably because the futures markets were overshadowed by widespread and aggressive marketing techniques used by early FX brokers to acquire new clients and gain speculative market share from futures brokers. Nonetheless, currency futures trade in abundance on the CME Group's Globex futures trading platform and arguably offer a more liquid trading environment than most give them credit for.

Similar to FX contracts, futures contracts are electronic agreements to make or take delivery of the underlying asset at a specific date in the future. In other words, the seller of a futures contract is agreeing to deliver the stated commodity on a predetermined delivery date; the buyer of a futures contract agrees to take delivery of the stated commodity at the stipulated delivery date. The only variable of a futures transaction is the price at which it is done—and buyers and sellers in the marketplace determine this. Traders often underestimate the stark difference between trading equities relative to trading in the leveraged environments of futures and FOREX. When a stock trader purchases a share of a certain company, he has bought an asset. As the owner of that stock he is entitled to any future cash flows produced by the stock, such as dividends and capital gains (assuming the stock is sold at a profit). FX and futures traders are not buying or selling an asset; instead they are trading a liability that is dependent, or derived, from the value of the underlying asset; thus, they are known as **derivatives.**

> Currency traders typically buy and sell contracts speculatively but have little interest in actually holding funds in denominations other than their home currency. Therefore, they roll over positions to avoid making or taking delivery of the underlying currency.

Unlike FX contracts, currency futures only go into delivery four times per year based on the quarterly cycle. If you recall, FX traders technically face delivery on positions held longer than two days but are required to roll over positions daily to avoid making or taking delivery. Currency futures traders, on the other hand, only have to worry about rolling over positions in March, June, September, and December. Rolling over simply entails offsetting an expiring contract and entering the next available contract month. For instance, a trader long a December Yen futures contract, with delivery of the underlying asset looming, would sell a December Yen to exit the position and buy a March Yen to reestablish a long position. Again, this process is known as *rolling over* and must be manually performed by the trader. This is unlike FOREX, where the brokerage automatically rolls over client positions.

Contract Expiration

By now, you know that futures contracts are expiring agreements between buyers and sellers of those contracts to exchange the underlying currency. You also know that most speculators have little interest in ever taking part in the delivery process. However, avoiding the delivery obligations involved in holding a futures contract is a bit more complicated than simply rolling over on the day before it officially expires.

Contract expiration is the day and time a particular delivery month of a currency futures contract ceases trading and the final settlement price is determined. This is when the delivery process begins. With the exception of a few somewhat obscure contracts, currency futures contracts listed on the CME Group go into delivery four times per year on the third Wednesday of March, June, September, and December. Assuming there isn't a holiday or other interference, the last trading day of CME currencies occurs on the Monday before expiration. Therefore, traders must be out of their positions well ahead of expiration. In fact, traders who aren't interested in making or taking delivery of the underlying currency must exit positions on the preceding Friday, but preferably earlier.

The CME publishes an official rollover date at which it recommends traders move positions from the expiring month to the next contract month. The suggested date to do this is exactly one week prior to the stated last trading day, and it probably doesn't hurt to beat the herd to the punch. You wouldn't want to hold open positions until the last trading day because the market will have likely thinned out by this time. Not only will this result in wider spreads between the bid and ask, but it could lead to irrational volatility.

To reiterate, FX rollovers take place daily, whereas futures rollovers only take place four times per year. Nonetheless, one of the advantages to trading in the FX market is that your broker will automatically roll over your positions without you lifting a finger. A futures brokerage won't give you the same courtesy, but if you are trading with a legitimate brokerage firm, it will do everything it can to notify you of contract expirations and prevent the delivery process from occurring. Although it might be one of the most common fears among futures traders, accidently holding positions into delivery is rare. If you make the mistake of triggering delivery, don't panic! It is fixable, but it might cost you a few hundred dollars to relinquish your obligation. Obviously, this is something you would ideally want to avoid.

Unlike FX rollovers, which involve the hassle and potential cost of interest rate differentials, futures traders don't have to be burdened with interest credits and debits. The only cost to rolling over a futures contract is the commission and the natural spread between the bid and ask prices, which is minimal (usually a tick).

Futures Markets Have High Standards

Without standardization of contracts, buyers and sellers would be forced to negotiate the details of each transaction. As you can imagine, this would slow the wheels of speculation tremendously and eliminate the liquidity and efficiency of the marketplace.

Despite significant differences in contract sizes between futures and FX, trading in both arenas utilizes standardized contracts that can be easily bought or sold in any order. In currency futures, there are three standard contract sizes. For instance, futures traders have the ability to trade a full-sized contract that ranges in size (with the exception of the Yen and the British Pound) from 100,000 to 125,000 units. A mini contract is sized at half of the standard, and the E-micro futures are one-tenth the size of the original futures contract.

How Can a Futures Exchange Guarantee Every Trade?

Once again, transactions in the FOREX market are subject to counterparty risk. If the person or entity taking the other side of your FX transaction is unable to meet his obligation, it is possible that you will not be compensated for accurate speculation; particularly if you are trading via a dealing desk in which your brokerage firm is acting as the market maker. As you can imagine, it might not always be in a position to meet its obligation in the trade. This is especially true should you manage to amass large profits because it could mean huge losses for the counterparty. Such events are rare in frequency, but I think we can all agree that once is too much! Just because it hasn't been a common issue in the past doesn't mean that it won't in the future—and it is hard to justify accepting unnecessary risks when it comes to trading. It's challenging enough to make money in the markets based on the controllable factors, let alone leaving the fate of your trading account up to the finances of others. An example of this is REFCO, the infamous U.S.-based FOREX broker that collapsed in 2005, thus turning the balances in client accounts to pennies on the dollar after the bankruptcy courts divvied up the leftovers.

One of the most attractive features of trading futures is the exchange guarantee. Each transaction cleared through a U.S. futures exchange is ensured; unfortunately, that guarantee isn't that you will make money. Instead, it is the assurance that if you do speculate correctly, you will be compensated in the amount deserved based on entry and exit price. Most traders assume this is always going to be the case regardless of the markets they trade and the broker they use, but it isn't. As discussed, FOREX traders are not afforded the same luxury of knowing the integrity of the market is always safeguarded by enforceable rules and regulations.

Although the NFA has more recently limited the leverage offered by FX brokers, in the past they were free to provide clients with hyper-leverage. As wonderful as some traders thought this to be, it is exactly why FX brokers could never guarantee trades; excessive leverage equates to more risk for *both* the counterparty and the trader. Futures exchanges stipulate and enforce margin requirements for each currency contract at a typically higher rate than similar contracts in FX. Doing so enables them the risk management necessary to provide traders with an execution guarantee.

Margin is a necessary evil; without ensuring that speculators have enough funds on deposit to cover potential losses, the exchanges and the futures brokerage firms, carry the risk of speculators simply walking away from their trading losses to leave them holding the bag. In fact, even with the required margin on deposit, it is possible for traders to lose more than the funds in their trading account (yes, this is possible with leveraged speculation and does happen). If this happens, it creates a negative client account balance, referred to as a **debit balance**, and results in a client that is indebted to his brokerage firm. Suddenly, the broker's role has shifted to creditor rather than merely the entity bringing buyers and sellers together. To further enable the futures exchange's ability to guarantee transactions, it is standard to hold the associated broker responsible for covering the client's obligations with the exchange until he is able to make the account whole again…if he ever is.

To illustrate the concept of leveraged investments and the power of margin, the real estate market in the late 2000s can be compared to a giant futures market without margin requirements and, even worse, without accountability. Government subsidies and aggressive mortgage techniques enabled many to purchase homes without any, or with very little, "margin" in the form of a down payment. We all know what happened next; some of those discovering they had purchased homes at unfavorable prices simply defaulted on their mortgage strategically to leave their counterparties (in this case, the banks) holding large losses with little hope for recourse. The result in some markets, such as my hometown of Las Vegas, was nothing short of chaos. I would imagine that a futures exchange without proper safeguards could be put in a similar situation should excessive market volatility strike.

Futures exchanges act as the bank by providing traders access to products with substantial value in return for a minimal "down payment" or margin. Luckily, actively enforced rules in regard to proper margining, and the fact that futures exchanges hold brokerage firms accountable for the debit balances of their clients, work toward market liquidity and (attempts at) stability—a characteristic that a marketplace without margin, such as real estate, might not always portray.

> "The numbers for successful guys are fleeting…because you are only as good as your last trade." —Joseph Gibbin (former floor trader), courtesy of the movie *Floored*

On the contrary, although FOREX traders seem to be less at risk of counterparty default in the current environment thanks to the NFA's new margin regulation that limits leverage to 50 to 1, this discrepancy between trading venues seems to make currency futures much more attractive relative to FX.

Now that we've made it clear that FOREX traders are subject to counterparty risk and futures traders aren't, let's look at the process that enables the futures exchanges to guarantee executed trades in a little more detail. As you know, to establish a position on a U.S. futures exchange, a trader must have a specific amount of margin on deposit. Should the trader's positions move adversely enough to trigger a margin call, then position adjustment, liquidation, or the deposit of funds is necessary to continue the speculative play.

If a futures trader fails to meet the requested margin requirement, the brokerage firm handling the account has the right to liquidate any positions as it sees fit in order to bring the account within exchange expectations. In the case of a trading account that has lost more money than was originally on deposit, positions are liquidated and the client is expected to bring the account whole by depositing funds to cover the debit account balance. Although futures exchanges guarantee each transaction, they aren't necessarily the party facing default risk; as mentioned, brokerage firms are held accountable for any negative balances in client accounts, at least until the client pays the monies owed. As we will soon find out, even brokerage firms pass the buck when it comes to responsibility of their clients. Because the exchanges themselves are the most critical entities in the futures industry, they are also the most protected when it comes to defaulting retail clients. Similarly, brokerage firms are somewhat safeguarded by their ability to hold individual brokers accountable; let's look at the particulars.

If the financial crisis of the late 2000s taught us anything, it is that not all members of society are always willing or able to meet their obligations. Accordingly, the individual broker handling the account is personally responsible in the form of commission withholding equal to the amount of the cash deficit. In other words, if a futures trading account loses more than is on deposit, the broker who brought the client to the firm—would not be paid commission on *any* of his accounts until enough money was withheld to offset the brokerage firm's liability to the exchange in the amount of the debit account balance. This is done because there is no guarantee the client will be able to meet his obligations; unfortunately for futures brokers like me, the possibility of client default is real and at times can be frustratingly costly.

Defaulting futures traders are not unlike consumers racking up credit card debt, only to walk away and leave the bank responsible for their spending spree. Obviously, there could be legal ramifications to follow, but in the meantime it is up to the brokerage firm, or more specifically the individual broker overseeing the account, to come up with the cash to keep the exchange happy.

> "Good trading is a peculiar balance between the conviction to follow your ideas and the flexibility to recognize when you have made a mistake."
> —Michael Steinhardt

In extreme cases, if the negative balance is large enough, the broker responsible for the client account might not make enough money to pay the deficit in a reasonable amount of time. In such scenarios, brokers sometimes opt to quit and undergo a career change, as opposed to working without compensation for a considerable period of time.

If this is the situation, the brokerage firm (no longer the broker) is responsible for ensuring that the cash to cover the debit is provided to the exchange. Only in the instance of a defaulting client, broker, and brokerage firm will the exchange be liable for losses in excess of funds on deposit. U.S. futures exchanges have established tiers of liability and, not surprisingly, they are at the top of the totem pole and this is exactly why they are comfortable guaranteeing each futures transaction. For those of us beneath the exchanges in the line of responsibility, it can seem unfair at times; but I think we all concur that the system encourages responsible trading by holding those proximal to the action accountable. Can you imagine if an entire futures exchange went bankrupt? The ripple effects could cripple the economy for decades; not only would speculators be subject to large losses, but large and small businesses hedging with futures and even consumers of commodities would suffer immensely. Luckily, exchange insolvency would only be possible if a trader, or traders, lost an incredibly substantial amount of money such that the broker, the brokerage, and the exchange were unable to cover the deficit.

The described accountability of risk and default creates an environment that attracts speculators and creates liquid and efficient markets for users and producers. With this known, those interested in entering the futures market as a broker, rather than a trader, must be willing to accept the nearly unlimited risk as well as the potential rewards.

FOREX traders, on the other hand, can certainly lose more money than is on deposit, but it is much less common simply because FX brokers are known for being far more proactive in force-liquidating client accounts than many futures brokers might be. In other words, futures brokers frequently give clients a courtesy call to clarify whether they will be able to wire funds to cover the margin deficit prior to blindly liquidating the account. Conversely, FX brokers tend to offset positions first and ask questions later; in fact, most FX trading platforms automatically liquidate client holdings once it is at risk of losing more than is on deposit. Perhaps the additional risk that comes with a lack of exchange guarantee has something to do with this.

Futures Bid/Ask Spread

All markets have a bid and ask spread; futures aren't an exception. However, unlike dealing desks in FX, which offer clients fixed bid/ask spreads, the futures markets involve free-floating bids and asks because currency futures traders are trading against other retail traders (or in some cases independent market makers), not their brokerage firm on a fabricated market. Simply put, futures contracts trade on a legitimate, transparent, and liquid marketplace. During peak hours, the spread between the bid and ask on the most liquid futures contracts is a single tick. However, in early evening trade, liquidity is less desirable and might be as high as three ticks. Either way, I believe futures contracts offer more efficient execution relative to trading with an FX dealing desk. That said, those trading with an ECN FX broker will enjoy attractive spreads and liquidity comparable to that of currency futures— or possibly even better.

Futures Margin

It should come as no surprise that futures margins are levied much differently than those in the FX market. After all, futures are traded on an organized exchange and face stiffer regulations; also, retail access to them has been in existence for decades. It is open for debate as to which arena offers the most efficient means of margin enforcement, but as a trader it isn't your job to analyze the rules. You just need to know them and make educated decisions accordingly.

On the surface, even in the aftermath of the NFA's new FOREX leverage limit of 50 to 1, it seems as though futures traders face much higher margin requirements and possibly get less bang for their buck in terms of leverage. However, determining this isn't as simple as looking at the dollar amounts required to hold positions in each market.

Unlike FOREX traders, who are subject to a single margin requirement, futures traders holding positions "overnight" are required to monitor two margin requirements: initial and maintenance. Day traders, on the other hand, have an entirely separate set of rules.

Who Determines Margin?

In the world of FOREX, the NFA determines leverage, and, therefore, margin rates for U.S. clients; but in futures trading it is the exchanges themselves that specify the margin required to hold a particular currency futures contract. However, what many fail to realize is that individual brokerage firms and brokers have the right to ask clients for additional funds to be on deposit. As discussed, because clients trading with leverage are at risk of losing more than what is on deposit, the brokerage firm is in a potentially compromising and expensive position should clients be unable to cover their losses. Accordingly, brokers have incentive to ask traders to deposit margin above and beyond exchange minimums to reduce risk of defaulting clients.

Those in witness of the historically excessive silver volatility during the spring of 2011 might recall one of the largest futures brokers in the nation dramatically increasing silver margin to over $20,000 from an exchange minimum at the time of about $12,000. Although it meant potentially upsetting clients, and likely reducing the trading volume at their brokerage, they felt as though the risks of providing access to the silver markets with anything less than a margin requirement of $20,000 to be too great to justify, despite a much lower margin stipulated by the exchange. Although it wasn't a popular move and was highly criticized by clients, as an industry insider, I felt like charging nearly twice the margin the exchange was asking for was completely justified; after all, a standard silver futures contract was moving $10,000 to $20,000 in a single trading day. Such an environment combined with the exchange minimum margin requirement of $12,000 opens the door for debit account balances to the tune of several thousand dollars. In the case of a client default of this magnitude, it isn't surprising to imagine that it would take a lot of commission for a brokerage firm to recover from such an event. Similar to the manner financial institutions adjust lending practices to manage their credit risk, futures brokerage firms must manage margin requirements to ensure they are protecting their ability to profit as well as remain viable.

To illustrate, let's look at a hypothetical example. If a trader paying $20 in commission goes negative $10,000 and is unable to pay the debit balance owed to the brokerage, it would take 500 round turns to bring in enough revenue to cover the loss, before considering clearing costs, operational costs, and so on. Even worse, if an individual broker is being held responsible, out of that $20 he might get $5 after paying the house; in this instance, the broker would have to execute 2,000 client round turns to get back into a position where he will actually earn commission—and not pay it. Please keep these realities in mind the next time your brokerage firm issues a margin call or asks that you avoid over-leveraging.

With that said, aside from extreme market conditions, such as the aforementioned silver scenario, futures traders are attracted to the arena by the availability of abnormally high leverage without the costs of borrowing securities or paying interest, as would be the case in a stock trading account. Accordingly, despite being an advocate of "leveraging down," I believe retail traders should be concerned with finding brokerage firms that generally margin their accounts based on exchange minimums. This is because even traders who attempt to use available margin conservatively could find themselves in the midst of a volatile and adverse price move. In such a case, the difference between exchange margin and the brokerage "up-charged" margin could mean the difference between receiving a margin call, and squeaking by without one, to avoid premature liquidation of positions.

Please note that although brokerage firms are free to charge margin in excess of exchange minimums, they are forbidden to decrease margin or allow undercapitalized traders to hold positions in the long term. As we will discuss, they do have the freedom to lower intraday margins for day traders.

How Is Futures Margin Determined?

Unlike FX margin, which is a single yet dynamic figure that constantly fluctuates based on the notional value of the contracts being traded, futures margin is relatively static. Although the exchange and brokerage firms have the right to increase, or decrease, margin requirements at any time, changes are typically infrequent. In some cases, several months or years might go by without an adjustment.

The premise of margin is to mitigate risk exposure to the exchange and brokerage firms by ensuring that traders have enough funds on deposit to cover losses that might reasonably be seen within a trading session. Accordingly, futures exchanges set margin rates based on current market volatility and not necessarily the nominal value of the contract, which is the dominant method in FOREX. If you recall, nominal value is the total worth of the currency contract when leverage is eliminated. However, as the nominal value increases, the futures exchanges tend to increase margin simply because, at higher prices, currencies tend to see larger price moves and expose traders to additional risk.

There is somewhat wide misconception of how currency futures margin is levied, so hopefully this explanation clears up some of the confusion. Exchange-stipulated margin doesn't come into play until the end of the trading session, which in the case of the CME currency futures is 4:00 p.m. Central. At this time, a snapshot of the account is taken and any open positions are margined accordingly; the status of the account at any other point in the day is nearly irrelevant in the eyes of the exchange.

Aside from the difference between variable and constant margin levies, another primary difference between futures and FX margin is the fact that futures margin includes two components: initial and maintenance.

Initial Margin

When traders refer to their futures margin requirement, they are referring to the **initial margin.** In other words, "initial margin" and "margin" are often used synonymously. In detail, initial margin is the amount of capital the exchange requires a trader to have on deposit to hold a given currency futures contract beyond the close of trade on the session the order was executed. For example, if the initial margin for a standard-sized Euro futures contract is $5,400, a trader should have at least this much in a trading account to execute a trade that is intended to be held overnight. Please note, as we will soon discuss in detail, day traders are not necessarily subject to the same requirements.

Maintenance Margin

The minimum account balance that must be maintained at the close of trade to avoid a margin call is known as the **maintenance margin.** Futures exchanges typically set the maintenance margin at about 70% to 80% of the initial margin.

Should an account balance dip below the maintenance margin requirement, as measured by the close of trade on any particular day, a margin call is generated and the trader is required to bring the account back above the initial margin. This can be done through position liquidation, adding funds to the trading account, or even mitigating margin using option hedges. Again, once an official margin call is triggered, it is no longer enough to bring the equity above the maintenance margin level; the account must meet the initial margin.

Keep in mind, a margin call is triggered only if the account is in violation at the close of a trading session. At any point intraday, it is nearly irrelevant. Therefore, it is quite possible for an account to experience a margin deficit in the middle of the trading day only to be off the hook by the close of trade, and vice versa. This differs from FOREX; FX traders are commonly issued intraday margin calls. This is because their margin requirement is being consistently measured as opposed to solely at the end of the trading day, as is the protocol in futures.

What Are Margin Calls?

Despite what the term implies, a **margin call** typically doesn't consist of a literal phone call from your broker; although in the recent past that was the case. Today, margin calls are typically communicated to traders via e-mail. The communication will state account details such as open positions, required initial and maintenance margin, the

---

margin deficiency, and current account value. In addition to a formal notice, brokerage firms display margin call details on the trader's daily statements, including the number of days the margin call has been active.

Futures brokers typically give traders two or three days to eliminate a margin call on their own accord, but each brokerage firm is different. Also, deep-discount brokers tend to be much less lenient when it comes to margin calls and forced account liquidation. I've witnessed several instances in which heavy-handed margin clerks at discount brokerages unnecessarily cost their clients large sums of money via arguably unjustified liquidation of positions. In a nutshell, a trader's quest to "save" money on commission sometimes results in dramatically increased peripheral costs—and these costs make a dollar or two in fees inconsequential. Like most things in life, up to a point, you will get what you pay for when it comes to transaction costs.

> Many discount brokers sacrifice margin leniency in dire situations, to keep costs and risk low. Paying a little more in commission is cheap when compared to the wrath of forced liquidation by heavy-handed margin clerks!

If a client goes one step beyond a simple margin call and is in danger of losing more than the funds on deposit, it is not uncommon for risk management clerks to force liquidate positions regardless of the brokerage firm and service type—and they have every right to do so. As a reminder, trading on leverage is identical to trading on credit. Similar to the credit-approval process for obtaining a credit card, brokerage firms reserve the right to revoke the right to trade on "credit." Similarly, as many discovered during the financial collapse of the late 2000s; credit is not a right, it is a privilege.

Day-Trading Margin Versus Overnight Margin

FOREX traders are required to maintain a certain margin level based on a specific leverage ratio. As you learned in Chapter 1, "What Is FOREX?," FX margin fluctuates with market prices and, more specifically, the nominal value of the pairs being traded. We've also determined that futures margins are relatively "fixed" and determined by the exchange. However, there is something we haven't touched on, and that is the difference between day-trading margin and overnight margin for futures traders.

In contrast to our previous discussion, which suggested traders must have the initial margin on deposit to enter a trade, there are exceptions for those who enter a trade based on the premise of offsetting their risk and obligation by the end of that particular trading session. For those traders engaged in the practice of day trading, brokerage firms, and even individual brokers, will often negotiate a discounted margin rate offering more leverage than is granted to traders who are holding positions overnight (as defined as beyond the close). For the purpose of margin, day trading is any activity in which trades are entered and exited within a single trading session. In today's world, the currency futures markets trade nearly 24 hours per day. Therefore, it is entirely possible for a trade to be entered in the evening, held overnight, and offset before the close of the day session to be treated as a "day trade." Conversely, although this trade was held "overnight," under the usual pretense of the phrase, both the entry and the exit occurred within a single trading session and, therefore, falls into the day-trading category in regard to margin. Many traders are surprised to discover that the futures exchange has very little say on the margin charged to clients for day-trading activity.

Depending on a trader's established relationship with his brokerage firm, or more importantly an individual broker, the margin charged on any intraday positions may be anywhere from 50% to 10% of the exchange's stipulated overnight rate. Naturally, only those clients believed to be responsible enough to have access to excessively low margin requirements are awarded the privilege; irresponsible traders are viewed as a credit risk to the brokerage and might not be granted the same freedoms. This is similar to the threats posed by those with low credit scores to a credit card company. With that said, as a means of risk management implemented by brokerage firms, some platforms are now capable of automatically liquidating accounts in danger of losing more than what is currently deposited. In the case of auto-liquidation, brokers might extend even more lenient margin policies to day traders simply because the luxury of auto-liquidation mitigates risk to the firm. Similar to the way a trader analyzes the market in terms of risk and reward, brokerage firms assess clients on a risk/reward basis and proceed accordingly. Brokerage revenue is commission based; they want you to trade, but not if it isn't worth the potential consequences.

Futures brokers who have auto-liquidate capabilities often ask clients to sign a disclosure statement acknowledging they are aware that positions might be offset without prior consent to the client if the account is deemed to be in danger of going negative—although they technically have the right to do so even without the agreement.

A common practice among futures brokers is to strategically place a stop order at a price that would prevent the account from losing more than is on deposit. However, as futures traders become more and more self-directed, this courtesy is slowly becoming less popular simply because in some ways it poses additional risk and potential liability to the broker. For example, "unruly" clients can easily cancel a stop order placed on their behalf to prevent a debit balance, and brokers simply don't have time to babysit accounts to ensure clients don't do so. In addition, if a stop order is placed for a specific number of contracts and the trader reduces the size of the position without adjusting the stop order, he might attempt to hold the brokerage firm liable for any erroneously resulting trades.

Thanks to highly discounted margin rates for day traders, it is possible for an account with little money on deposit but always exits positions before the close, to trade well above and beyond the stated margin level without ever receiving a margin call. For instance, a trader with an account balance of $1,000 might be granted permission by the broker to day-trade one Euro currency futures contract despite the fact that the overnight margin requirement is upward of $5,400. In fact, in extreme cases brokerage firms have been known to extend discounted margins to traders to the tune of 5% to 10% of the overnight rate. Thus, assuming an exchange-stipulated margin of $5,400, a trader may be able to buy or sell a Euro currency futures contract with as little as $270, assuming that she exits the position by the close of trade—or doesn't run out of money beforehand. Take into account that although it is not a good idea to trade with so much leverage, overly aggressive traders have been known to frequently abuse the privilege as a result of the freedom to do so.

Bear in mind that many of the deep-discount brokerage firms do not allow clients to enjoy discounted day-trading margins during "off" hours, or in overnight trading. Instead, they are available only during what the brokerage determines as the day session; 7 a.m. to 2 p.m. Central for most, or in some cases 7 a.m. to 4 p.m. Central. This is just another example of "getting what you pay for." Sometimes, cheap commission isn't as cheap as it seems on the surface. It makes perfect sense: Brokerage firms that charge a little more in commission can justify giving their clients a longer leash because the additional revenue slightly offsets some of the risk involved in taking on a new client.

The Bottom Line

Thanks to the standardization of contracts, the subsequent ease of buying or selling them, and a lack of default risk, futures trading has attracted mass price speculation. Participation is no longer limited to those who own, or would like to own, the underlying currency; instead, unrelated third parties can easily involve themselves in the markets in hopes of accurately predicting, and thus profiting from, price fluctuations.

> "Now, in any market, a group of men reasoning with the same facts often arrive at varying conclusions because they do not give the same weight to each of the facts."
> —Arthur W. Cutten

For reasons highlighted throughout this chapter, I feel as though the futures markets offer traders a more transparent marketplace, with lower costs, less peripheral risks, and favorable integrity. That said, each trader must weigh the facts and choose a venue based on her personal circumstances and opinions.

7

Calculating in Currency Futures

A s a reminder, unlike FX pairs in which the Dollar might or might not be the quote currency, currency futures are, for the most part, traded in "American terms." Using FX lingo, this simply means that the USD is the quote currency and the prices listed in the futures market represent the Dollar price of each foreign currency. This translates into the cost in U.S. Dollars of the foreign currency. In order to understand the point of view of the futures price, ask yourself "How much of our currency does it take to buy one theirs?"

Because currency futures are all (with the exception of the new line of E-micro futures discussed later in the chapter and a handful of less-traded contracts) paired against the U.S. Dollar in American terms (USD as the quote currency), calculating profit and loss is as easy as multiplying the number of ticks in price movement by a constant multiplier. Hence, there is no need to convert anything back to the home currency—it is already in terms of the greenback. Because of this, and the fact that futures margins are relatively constant (as opposed to floating based on the nominal value of the contract), I find currency futures much easier to deal with and I believe the math a little less intimidating to newer traders. That said, the tick value per currency varies from contract to contract due to differences in contract size.

Rules to Simplify Calculating Profit and Loss in Futures

Although calculating profit and loss in futures is a bit less complicated than doing so in FX, it can be a tricky task. I've come up with a couple rules to guide you in doing so.

Rule # 1: Use Multipliers, Not Contract Sizes

Ultimately, there are two manners in which traders can accurately determine the Dollar amount of profit, loss, and risk in futures trading. Most sources tend to suggest beginning traders use contract sizes in their figuring, but in my opinion it might be beneficial to use contract multipliers instead. This is because doing so typically involves smaller numbers, less confusion over decimals and fractions, and hopefully less room for error.

For our purposes, a **multiplier** is simply the Dollar value of a specific price move in the underlying commodity. In the case of currencies, I recommend using the minimum tick value, which ranges from $10 to $12.50 for most futures contracts but is $6.25 for the British Pound. Using ticks to calculate in futures is similar to working with pips in FOREX and therefore should be a moderately comfortable task. As you can imagine, using such figures in your math work could be less cumbersome than using contract sizes, which range from 12,500,000 Yen to 62,500 British Pounds. In addition, it's likely easier to remember the multiplier in the Yen is $12.50 as opposed to remembering that the contract size is 12,500,000.

With that said, it is necessary to realize that each of the conclusions reached using multipliers can also be achieved through an alternative calculation involving contract size. In the case of the Euro, it is easy to see that the $12.50 multiplier is the result of multiplying the contract size by a single tick (125,000 × 0.0001) and therefore either $12.50 or 125,000 could be used to determine the value of a futures price change. However, for reasons I will soon point out, doing so seems to create confusion, not solve it.

Rule # 2: Stay "Positive"

I believe it's beneficial for traders to work with positive values; negative figures often create confusion and breed calculation errors. For that reason, traders should always be subtracting the smaller number from the larger number to derive a positive value. This means that before a calculation begins, you should determine whether it was a profit or a loss; this might come across as obvious, but it's important to fully understand the concept. Currency traders often have to make quick calculations in the heat of the moment, and mistakes or delays can be costly.

Obviously, the goal is to buy a currency futures contract low and sell it high, or sell it high and buy it low; if this is accomplished, the trade yields a profit. On the other hand, doing the exact opposite (buying high and selling low) will always result in a net loss. Once it is determined whether the trade is positive or negative, it is possible to easily subtract the smaller price from the larger price to determine the magnitude of the result and apply that number to the win or loss column accordingly.

Although several currency futures contracts are listed on the CME, we will only discuss the most commonly traded: the Euro, Franc, Yen, British Pound, Canadian Dollar, and Australian Dollar (see Table 7-1).

Table 7-1   The Most Commonly Traded Futures Contracts

Contract	Multiplier	Contract Size	Minimum Tick Value	Symbol
Euro	$12.50	125,000 Euro	$12.50 (1 tick)	6E
Swiss Franc	$12.50	125,000 Swiss Francs	$12.50 (1 tick)	6S
Yen	$12.50	12,500,000 Yen	$12.50 (1 tick)	6Y
British Pound	$6.25	62,500 British Pounds	$6.25 (1 tick)	6B
Canadian Dollar	$10	100,000 Canadian Dollars	$10 (1 tick)	6C
Australian Dollar	$10	100,000 Australian Dollars	$10 (1 tick)	6A
Dollar Index	$10	$1,000 × index value	$5 (0.5 tick)	DX

NOTE

Futures traders might find it most convenient to use the contract multiplier, known as a **tick** to futures traders but is equivalent to a pip in FX, to derive profit, loss, and risk. However, contract size can also be used.

Calculating in the Euro, Swiss Franc, and Yen Futures

In many ways, calculating profit, loss, and risk in futures trading is much easier than the challenges faced by FX traders. Although various futures contracts have slightly different tick values, their values are constant and the profit and loss of a trade never has to be converted to U.S. Dollars… because they already are. If you recall, currency futures are all quoted in "American terms," which means the greenback is *always* the quote currency because prices are *always* stated in the number of Dollars it takes to purchase the foreign currency.

Although they are backed by dramatically different fundamentals and histories, the Euro, Yen, and Swiss Franc futures have identical profit, loss, and risk calculations. Each of these currencies has a minimum tick value of $12.50, which I recommend traders use as the multiplier when doing trading math. Accordingly, for each tick the price of these futures moves, a trader makes or loses $12.50, and because the profit and loss are already quoted in U.S. dollars, there is no need to waste time converting to the home currency.

To demonstrate, if the June Euro futures contract is trading at 1.4550, it is equivalent to saying that a single Euro could be purchased for $1.4550 (in other words, one Dollar and forty-five and a half cents buys one Euro). The convenience of knowing each tick is worth $12.50 means traders can ignore the decimal to simplify the math. Although $12.50 may not seem like much, it adds up quickly. For instance, if the Euro futures contract travels from 1.4550 to 1.4551, a trader short the future would have lost $12.50 and a trader on the long side would have made $12.50. Similarly, if the price changes to 1.4853, the trade would be a winner or loser (depending on the side of the market you are on) in the amount of 303 ticks (1.4853 − 1.4550) or $3,787.50 (303 × $12.50). Although I believe it to produce more grunt work, and most likely errors, the same answer can be calculated using contract sizes. As an illustration, 303 ticks is equivalent to 3.03 cents, or 0.0303 (1.4853 − 1.4550), and the standard contract size for the Euro futures is 125,000 (125,000 × 0.0303 = $3,787.50).

As mentioned, the Swiss Franc shares the same contract size and tick value characteristic as the Euro; many traders refer to this contract simply as the "Franc." Prior to the Euro, the Franc was a widely traded futures contract. However, in the current environment the volume traded in the Swiss Franc is a fraction of that seen in the Euro.

The Mysterious Yen

Despite the fact that they all share the same tick value ($12.50), the contract size of the Yen futures contract is vastly different from that of the Euro and the Swiss Franc. Each standard futures contract in the Euro and the Frank represents 125,000 units of the underlying currency. However, a Yen futures contract represents 12,500,000. This is because the value of a single Yen is nearly worthless and can be thought of similarly to a penny in U.S. currency. In other words, if the U.S. Dollar didn't exist and all of our transactions took place in pennies, the U.S. currency would trade nearly equally to the Yen. You might see the Yen *futures* contract quoted at a rate of 1.2240. Unlike the Euro, this does not mean it would cost $1.224 Dollars to buy a single Yen. Instead, it can be looked at in two ways: the "price" of a Yen is 1.224 cents, or the cost of 100 Yen is $1.224.

In addition to the difference in the manner the Yen is quoted and priced relative to the other major currency futures, the Yen causes many beginning traders confusion due to differences in the way it is valued in the futures market relative to the FX market.

There are two primary differences between Yen futures and the USD/JPY FX pair that create what appears to be diverse pricing for the Yen; yet, in both markets, the currency's inherent value will always be similar. For starters, Yen futures and the Dollar/Yen currency pair in FOREX are quoted in inverse terms (to be explained later). Secondly, FX contracts represent immediate delivery and futures represent "future" delivery, which causes some variation in pricing. Nonetheless, for now our focus will be on the terms in which prices are displayed in each market. Please note that the Canadian Dollar futures and the USD/CAD currency pair are also quoted inversely in each arena.

We recognize the value of each futures contract, including the Yen, is priced and traded in terms where the Dollar is the quote currency; therefore, the foreign currency is the base currency. Plainly, futures traders view currency values in terms of what the price of any particular currency is in U.S. Dollars.

As discussed in Chapter 2, "Making 'Cents' of Currency Pairs," the Yen is traded against the greenback in the FOREX markets using the standard USD/JPY pair, where the Dollar is the base currency and the Yen the quote currency. This is the exact opposite to the terms the Yen is traded in the futures market; the CME's Yen futures are paired against the Dollar and are in terms of the Dollar. If the CME's futures contract were listed as a pair, it would be expressed as JPY/USD. As you can see, it is the inverse of the FX version. Therefore, prices in each of these venues will be inverse of each other. To clarify even further, in the futures market, traders are quoting the price of the Yen in terms of the Dollar, but in FX, traders are quoting the price of the Dollar in Yen.

Accordingly, the USD/JPY in the FX market will be trading in the 80s while the Yen futures contract (essentially the JPY/USD, if there were such a thing) will be trading in the 1.20s. For instance, assume a Yen futures value of 1.2240; this is the equivalent to 1 Yen/1.2240 (JPY/USD) or, in other words, 1 Yen is equal to 1.2240 cents. The inverse of this can be found by dividing 1 by 1.2240 (1/1.2240), or 0.8169. In FOREX, however, you will see the Yen quoted with two digits on the right of the decimal, such as 81.69. When the decimal is moved, the price is now quoted in the cost per 1 U.S. Dollar. In other words, 81.69 Yen are required to purchase 1 U.S. Dollar.

Before you go and verify the math by taking the inverse of the current futures price and attempting to compare it to the going spot rate in the FX market, keep in mind that it likely won't be a perfect match. Adding to the complexity, unlike the USD/JPY currency pair in FOREX, which is deliverable to the trader within two days, Yen futures are priced for *future* delivery (as the title of the contract implies). To recap, the FX market is known as the spot market because delivery of the underlying asset is set to occur nearly immediately should a trader fail to "roll" her contracts to a distant delivery date (usually the next day). Yen futures expire quarterly, so the value of a futures contract might reflect market expectations of the Yen three months in the future, more or less.

Aussie and Canadian Dollars

The Aussie and the Canadian have a strong tendency to move in tandem with commodity prices; for this reason they are often referred to as the "commodity currencies." Because each of these futures has a standard contract size of 100,000 units, the tick value and multiplier is $10. Accordingly, for every tick a trader gains or loses, he will experience a profit or loss of $10.

In recent years, the Aussie Dollar has been highly volatile, and due to massive gains in commodity prices, the currency nearly doubled in value from 2008 through 2011. Nonetheless, a trader who goes short the June Aussie Dollar futures contract at 1.0534 and places a buy stop at 1.0634 is risking $1,000. This can easily be figured by dropping the decimal and multiplying the difference between the entry and exit price by $10—that is, (10534 – 10634) × $10.

At a rate of 1.0634, it requires $1.06 "and change" to purchase a single Aussie Dollar; however, in 2008, you might have seen a quote of 0.8832. Even though there wasn't a digit on the right side of the quote, the math is performed in the same manner. Therefore, if a trader sells an Aussie future at 0.8832 and then later buys it back at 0.8811, she would have made $210—that is, (8832 – 8811) × $10.

British Pound

In the futures markets, the British Pound is in a world of its own. Both its contract size and tick value are dramatically different from the other foreign currencies. A standard British Pound futures contract trades in the size of 62,500 units; as a result, the tick value and multiplier are $6.25. You might have noticed that the contract size and tick value of the British Pound are exactly half that of the Euro and the Swiss Franc. Nevertheless, the process of figuring profit, loss, and risk is identical. For instance, if the December British Pound futures contract is priced at 1.6178, it costs exactly $1.6178 to purchase a single unit. A trader long from the current price with a limit order to lock in a profit at 1.6248 is hoping to make $437.50 on the trade. This can be figured by dropping the decimals and multiplying the difference in entry and exit by $6.25— that is, (16178 – 16248) × $6.25.

It seems logical to assume that because the British Pound future carries a smaller contract size and tick value that it would be a "tamer" place for speculation. In some cases, this might be true, but you shouldn't take this market for granted. I have personally witnessed a single trading session in which the British Pound futures market traded in an approximate range of 1,000 points, or $6,250 per contract.

Diversity of the Dollar Index

The relative oddball of the currency futures complex is, without a doubt, the U.S. Dollar Index. However, just because it is different from the others doesn't mean that traders should be put off by it. In fact, this particular futures contract offers something that is relatively rare in most other futures contracts—diversity.

The Dollar Index was originally the product of the NYBOT (New York Board of Trade) but in recent years has been acquired by the Intercontinental Exchange, more commonly known as ICE. According to the exchange, the U.S. Dollar Index futures contract is a leading benchmark for the international value of the U.S. Dollar and the world's most widely recognized traded currency index—and I'd have to agree with it. Unlike the other currencies we have discussed that are paired against the U.S. Dollar and are quoted in "American" terms, the DX is the value of the U.S. Dollar against a basket of foreign currencies. This futures contract enables traders to speculate on the value of the Dollar in general, as opposed to against a specific currency. The Dollar Index futures contract might also be used to hedge currency risk within an international stock, bond, and perhaps even commodity portfolio.

In addition, I feel as though the U.S. Dollar Index futures contract should be seen as an alternative vehicle to the highly volatile metals complex. For instance, many investors in silver and gold are of the opinion that a declining Dollar offers strong incentives to own currency alternatives such as precious metals. However, as many such investors have discovered, or abruptly learned the hard way, the metals trading arena can be treacherous. Even in the most bullish of markets, corrections can be swift and fierce. For instance, in May of 2011, silver futures fell nearly 30% in a matter of a few trading days after reaching a fresh multi-decade high (see Figure 7-1). Rather than pushing your luck in metals, perhaps a more efficient, and possibly tamer, trade would simply be to short the DX futures contract.

> "The worse a situation becomes, the less it takes to turn it around, the bigger the upside."
> —George Soros

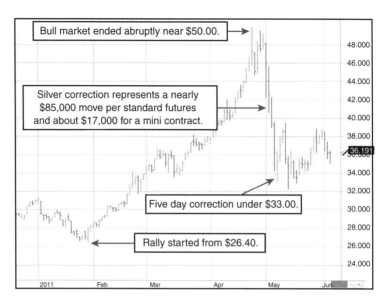

Charting software courtesy of QST.

Figure 7-1 Dollar bulls and bears often turn to the metals market for speculation, but perhaps a more efficient and less volatile venue is the U.S. Dollar Index futures traded on the ICE exchange.

The Dollar Index was introduced in 1973, and its composition has only been changed once; in January 1999 the Euro was launched to replace a number of European currencies, such as the Italian Lira, the Greek Drachma, the French Franc, and Deutsche Mark, among seventeen others. Because the Euro represents multiple countries and is the most commonly traded currency against the U.S. Dollar, it makes up 57.6% of the Dollar Index. The second largest represented currency in the index is the Japanese Yen at 13.6% (see Figure 7-2).

The inherent diversity built into the U.S. Dollar Index futures traded on ICE helps to mitigate the overall volatility of the contract. Although the foreign currencies tend to be highly correlated in that on days when the dollar is higher, the Yen, Euro, Pound, Canadian, and other futures have a tendency to all be lower to various degrees, this isn't always the case. For instance, in early 2011 there were times when the Euro and the Yen futures (paired against the greenback) moved in the opposite direction. Similarly, even if these foreign currencies are moving together, some might only see moderate price changes while others are experiencing much larger moves. In other words, the index itself eliminates some of the country-specific event risk, and works toward smoothing out market volatility that traders might be exposed to if choosing undiversified products such as the Euro or Yen futures contract.

U.S. Dollar Index

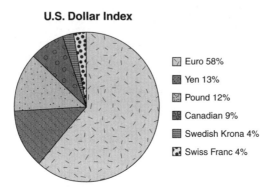

Euro 58%

Yen 13%

Pound 12%

Canadian 9%

Swedish Krona 4%

Swiss Franc 4%

Figure 7-2   The U.S. Dollar Index traded via the Intercontinental Exchange offers traders a diversified trading product.

Thanks to diversification and theoretically mitigated volatility relative to most other currency futures, the Dollar Index requires a moderate amount of margin to hold a position overnight. At the time of this writing, ICE required traders to have $1,197 on deposit (initial margin) and only $900 to maintain the position (maintenance margin). To put this into perspective, the initial margin on the standard-sized Euro and Yen futures were $5,400 and the Canadian Dollar was $2,430.

Also setting Dollar Index futures apart from the rest is the manner in which contract size is determined. In the case of the foreign currency futures, contract size is predetermined by the exchange and remains constant. For instance, we now know the standard Euro futures on the CME has a contract size of 125,000 Euro, but the Canadian Dollar futures trade at a size of 100,000. The DX, on the other hand, is an index and, therefore, the size is determined by the value of the index. This is similar to other futures contracts such as the S&P 500 and the Dow Jones that represent an index rather than a single underlying asset with a specified quantity.

The size, or nominal value, of the Dollar Index futures is determined by multiplying $1,000 by the index value. For example, if the June DX is trading at 76.00, the contract size would be $76,000; similarly, if the Dollar Index is trading at 82.45, the contract size is $82,450. You will find that the contract size and the nominal value will be identical when referring to indices; this is because you aren't trading in quantities but in relative values.

As if the Dollar Index wasn't unique enough, since taking over the contract the ICE exchange has begun trading Dollar Index futures in half-ticks. Simply, instead of the minimum price movement being .01, it is now .005. For instance, if the index is trading at 81.500, the price can go up by 0.005 to 81.505 or down to 81.495. Because the 0.005 represents a half tick, it is valued at $5 rather than the $10 tick value. The additional digit often causes confusion when it comes to calculating profit, loss, and risk because simply looking at the quote board it is impossible to determine that the last digit of the quote is actually a fraction of a tick—specifically a half of a tick.

In my opinion, the easiest way to calculate in the Dollar Index is to move the decimal place in the quote to the last digit that represents a whole integer and do the math from there. In a nutshell, this means shifting the decimal in the quote two places to the right.

Let's take a look at an example. A trader who purchases the December DX futures at 82.255 (82.25 and a half) and places a limit order to take a profit at 83.150 and a stop order at 81.000, has a profit target of $895—that is, (8315.0 – 8225.5) × $10—and is attempting to limit his losses on the trade to $1,255—that is, (8225.5 – 8100) × $10. As shown in the calculations, by shifting the decimal two places to the right, the trader simply needs to multiply the sum of the entry and exit prices by $10 (the multiplier).

E-micro Currency Futures

The CME Group listed its E-micro FOREX futures in an attempt to lure smaller speculators away from FX and into the world of futures. The CME Group itself is the largest regulated currency marketplace in the world. However, the E-micro futures aren't incredibly liquid just yet. That said, there are fabulous market makers who keep spreads attractive at all times of the day. Accordingly, don't let the claims of substantial liquidity in FOREX deter you from futures. When it comes to FX liquidity, there is a lot of smoke and mirrors, but with futures there is true transparency and in many cases better trade execution—and that is what really matters anyway.

We'll focus on the EUR/USD E-micro futures because the relationship between the Euro and the Dollar is the most watched, traded, and referred to. The EUR/USD E-micro future has a tick value of $1.25 rather than the $12.50 that comes with holding a standard-sized contract (remember, tick values on futures contracts are constant, but pip values in FX are variable if the USD is not the quote currency). To clarify, the E-micro FOREX futures are exactly 1/10th the size of the original-sized futures contract.

The CME Group's E-micro futures contracts offer lower margin (and therefore lower risk) alternatives to retail traders (see Table 7-2).

Table 7-2   The CME Group's E-micro Futures Contracts

Contract	Multiplier	Contract Size	Minimum Tick Value	Symbol
EUR/USD	$1.25	12,500 Euros	0.0001 USD/EUR ($1.25)	M6E
USD/JPY	100 Yen (converted to $)	10,000 USD	0.01 JPY/USD (100 Yen) (Approx. $1)	M6J
JPY/USD	$1.25	1,250,000 JPY	0.000001 USD/JPY	MJY
GBP/USD	$0.625	6,250 British Pounds	0.0001 USD/GBP ($0.625)	M6B
CAD/USD	$1.00	10,000 CAD	0.0001 USD/CAD ($1)	MCD
USD/CAD	1 CAD (converted to $)	10,000 USD	0.0001 CAD/USD (Approx. $1)	M6C
AUD/USD	$1.00	10,000 AUD	0.0001 USD/AUD ($1)	M6A
USD/CHF	1 CHF (converted to $)	10,000 USD	0.0001 CHF/USD (Approx. $1)	M6S
CHF/USD	$1.25	12,500 CHF	0.0001 USD/CHF	MSF

A trader who is making or losing $1.25 per tick will have a much easier time (mentally and financially) adding to the position should the market move adversely and will have better odds of avoiding a margin call. At the time of this writing, the Euro was valued at about $1.4800, much higher than the $1.1800 seen in the summer of 2010, which was supposedly the "beginning of the end" for the Euro according to some gurus. In the middle of 2010, most TV, Internet, and newspaper commentators were pointing toward the Euro trading at par with the dollar (at

1.0000) or even the European Union being disbanded making the Euro essentially worthless. On the other hand, the all-time high in the Euro is considerably higher, near $1.6000. If you haven't done the math yet, the range between what are two historically extreme prices in the Euro represents about $7,500 to a Micro-FX futures contract trader. No doubt, this is a good deal of money, but when compared to a standard-sized Euro futures contract, where the range calculates to $75,000, it appears to be a much tamer speculative venture and, consequently, to offer better odds of success.

Futures and FOREX Fees Side by Side

The process of determining whether to trade currencies in the futures or FOREX markets can be a frustrating and overwhelming task. Unfortunately, aggressive marketing efforts by FX firms, pushy salesman on both sides of the argument, and maybe even peer pressure can make it difficult for traders to look at the larger picture when it comes to transaction costs. Now that you are familiar with the futures markets, we can briefly compare the transaction costs in each trading arena.

Futures traders are charged a set round turn commission by their brokerage firm but are also liable for exchange fees and possible platform and GLOBEX fees. GLOBEX is the electronic trade matching program used by the CME Group to facilitate order execution, and round turn implies entering *and* exiting the position. Although the commission is negotiable, exchange and GLOBEX fees are not. As a result, traders should expect their round turn cost to be $2.00 to $3.00 above and beyond the commission charged. Therefore, a trader paying $15 round turn in commission and assuming an additional $3.00 in exchange fees would face a total charge of $9.00 (($15/2) + ($3/2)) on the way in and $9.00 on the way out (these figures are rounded for simplicity). Some traders agree to pay their brokers more, and others less, but you get the idea. Don't forget, futures traders also pay a hidden cost in the form of the bid/ask spread which is typically a tick; this adds another $12.50 to the total cost of a single contract. With this assumed commission rate, the complete cost to execute a futures contract is about $30.50 ($15 + $3 + $12.50). Please note, most self-directed futures traders are likely paying a lower commission rate.

As we've discussed, a trader using a dealing-desk brokerage firm doesn't pay any commission or transaction fee at all but is subject to a bid/ask spread of 3 to 5 ticks on most of the major currency pairs. Each currency can have a different pip value, but we know they are typically around $10. Accordingly, what is marketed as commission free trading actually involves a hidden cost of somewhere between $30 and $50 per standard lot, per trade.

Those trading with an ECN broker face much tighter pip spreads—sometimes equivalent to a pip or less. However, they are charged a "mark-up" for access to the ECN that is typically in the vicinity of $10 on the way in and $10 on the way out. Thus, assuming a pip spread of 1, the total in and out cost to a non-dealing desk client is about $30.

As you can see, despite vastly different methods of generating transaction fees from clients, each trading venue exposes traders to similar costs. Ironically, the so called commission free venue likely carries the highest trading fees.

Table 7-3 offers a side-by-side comparison of the fee structure for each market and broker type. Although futures fees are more obvious, they might actually be lower.

Table 7-3   Side-by-Side Comparison of the Fee Structure for Each Market and Broker Type

	FOREX	Non-Dealing-Desk FOREX	Currency Futures
Commission	No	Yes	Yes
Fixed spread	Yes, higher than the actual interbank spread	No, variable based on liquidity	No, variable based on liquidity
Exchange fees	No	No	Yes
Platform fees	No	No	Yes
GLOBEX fee	No	No	Yes

8

Currency ETFs Versus
FOREX and Futures

xchange Traded Funds, commonly known as ETFs, are
investment funds that trade as equities. Unlike typical mutual
funds, which can only be bought or sold based on settlement
prices at the end of a trading day, ETFs can be bought or sold throughout
the day just like a share of stock. ETFs began as a tool to trade stock
indices, such as the S&P 500, and offered an alternative to actively
managed equity funds that come with hefty management fees. However,
as the industry progressed and investor demand for alternative assets
has grown, ETFs have become a hot bed of commodity and currency
speculation.

I won't pretend to be an expert in this field. I am a futures, options, and
FOREX broker and, therefore, that is where my comfort lies. However,
I wouldn't be doing this book justice by skipping the third asset class
used by currency traders. With that said, it is also fair to say that
although the opinions expressed in this text are believed to be sound and
justifiable, some might argue that my opinion could be biased based on
my background. Nonetheless, I feel that is my job to give you as much
information as I see it, and leave it up to you to make the decision for
your own circumstances.

What Are Currency ETFs?

Currency ETFs track the value of a single foreign currency, a basket of
currencies, or even the U.S. Dollar via cash bank deposits in alternative
currencies *or* futures contracts. Within those currency ETFs in which
gains and losses are determined by holdings in the futures market, fund

managers typically purchase Treasury securities to be used as margin. This is because most futures brokerage firms will accept T-bills and short-term notes as margin collateral, as opposed to depositing cash. In most cases, about 95% of the T-bill value can be used toward margin and moderately less can be used for short-term notes.

Although some ETFs use futures for their currency exposure, the leverage is typically stripped by overfunding; the exceptions to this are ETFs, which stipulate leverage and require a margin deposit (such funds are labeled as double or triple leverage).

To keep things simple, we'll assume a currency ETF is trading a single futures contract (but in reality currency ETFs hold futures positions in massive volume). Assume an ETF manager purchases a single contract of the June Dollar Index at $75.73. The nominal value of the contract is $75,730 (7,573 × $10) but the actual margin is only $1,200. However, depending on the fund's purpose or intended leverage ratio, there is likely much more on deposit than the required margin. Assuming a zero leverage fund, the fund manager could keep about $75,000 in cash on deposit or she could purchase $79,000 ($75,000 × 1.05) worth of Treasury bills to margin the position. Don't forget, only 95% of the T-bill value can be used toward margin, so a bit of additional capital is required.

Obviously, the benefit of margining positions with T-bills is the incremental income to the fund in the form of interest payments. When interest rates are historically low (as was the case at the time of this writing), the proceeds are nearly inconsequential, but in more normal financial market scenarios the interest proceeds work toward paying the fund managers (making the ETF relatively self-sufficient). If rates are high enough, they even return a small profit to investors. Naturally, if the futures positions the T-bills are margining move adversely, the interest income likely won't seem like a valid consolation prize.

You might also run across what are known as ETNs, or Exchange Traded Notes. These are non-interest-paying debt instruments whose value fluctuates with the underlying currency exchange rate. However, because they are debt obligations, they are subject to default risk by the issuer and therefore might not be an optimal choice.

Which ETFs Are Available?

The ETF market is constantly evolving to add additional products, so providing you with an exhaustive list isn't practical. Similarly, many of the ETFs available are relatively new, and therefore in many cases illiquid; accordingly, it isn't productive to introduce traders to products that haven't matured enough to provide ample opportunity to trade them efficiently. Nonetheless, Table 8-1 provides a list of the rather popular currency ETFs.

Table 8-1   Some Popular Currency ETFs

ETF	Name	Currency
FXA	Currencyshares Australian $	Australian Dollar
FXC	Currencyshares Canadian $	Canadian Dollar
FXS	Currencyshares Swedish Krona	Swedish Krona
FXB	Currencyshares British Pound	British Pound
FXE	Currencyshares Euro Trust	Euro
FXF	Currencyshares Swiss Franc	Swiss Franc
UUP	Powershares Bullish U.S. $	U.S. Dollar
UDN	Powershares Bearish U.S. $	U.S. Dollar

NOTE

Currency equity products have been created to prevent speculative capital from moving to the futures and FX markets, but the convenience of trading currencies within a stock account comes with glaring disadvantages.

In addition to these, there are ETFs based on more exotic currencies, such as the Brazilian Real and the Indian Rupee. However, just as I don't necessarily feel like the average speculator belongs in such products in the futures and FX markets, I doubt they are the best choice for retail equity ETF traders. Furthermore, some listed ETFs provide traders with leverage or attempt to mimic the opposite payout of the underlying currency, or even both. For example, ticker symbol DRR represents a security that provides "double" short Euro exposure to traders. However, as discussed next, there are substantial drawbacks to using leveraged or inverse (short) equity instruments.

The Good and Bad of Currency ETFs

Currency ETFs can be rather complex instruments, and their value is often determined by much more than the underlying currency price. Accordingly, currency ETFs are not necessarily attractive for long-term investors. Many ETFs, especially leveraged and "short" versions, are designed to mimic the direction of the underlying currency within a single trading session or two. However, over the span of weeks and months, traders holding positions in the ETFs might notice that their profits and losses (in terms of percentages) are dramatically different from the change of the currency in question. Thus, while some might consider these viable vehicles for day traders, they are an extremely inefficient means of position trading. In my opinion, it doesn't make sense to trade products that are intended to mimic others—to me it makes more sense to go to the original product in the first place. After all, why buy one asset because you want to sell another? Trading leveraged and short ETFs can be compared to eating imitation crab; it looks and feels like crab, but it definitely isn't as satisfying as the real deal!

> Never be afraid to try something new. Remember, amateurs built the ark, professionals built the Titanic.

Frankly, ETFs seem to be one of the least efficient means of speculating in currencies. Nonetheless, it is popular simply because people have a tendency to go with what they are comfortable with, and equity products are much more widely traded among retail traders than FX and futures. Similarly, it is extremely convenient to trade equity products given the fact that most people now have online access to a stock trading or investment account in which currency ETFs can be easily traded. That said, convenience isn't a substitute for due diligence.

Along with familiarity and convenience, another argument for trading currency ETFs (although not necessarily a valid one) is the lack of complex math. Unlike futures contracts, which have various tick values per product or FX contracts in which pip values fluctuate with exchange rates, the profit and loss calculations in currency ETFs is cut and dry. Each share purchased makes or loses exactly the difference between the entry and exit price. For example, if you buy 1 share of UUP at $21.35 and sell it at $22.35, you have made $1—no ifs, ands, or buts. If you traded 100 shares, the profit would be $100 ($1.00 × 100). Clearly, there are no smoke and mirrors here; it is easy to see why the average investor might relate to currency ETFs more than other trading arenas.

Aside from the obvious drawback to trading ETFs (that is, trading synthetically created products rather than the "real thing"), there are other reasons why ETFs might not be the optimal choice. For one, they do not provide traders with the option of leverage without either compromising efficiency or borrowing shares and paying interest. As mentioned, both the futures and FX arenas grant traders a great deal of free leverage, and although I don't always advocate using it to the maximum degree, it is nice to have the flexibility to do so.

In addition, I argue that currency ETFs are considerably more expensive to trade. Not only does each fund come with what is normally a high management fee, but on top of that traders must pay a commission getting in and out of the fund itself. Although commission is involved in futures and FOREX trading, there aren't fund management fees. This is one instrument where I agree that you might not get what you pay for.

Unfortunately, the human tendency to be a creature of habit often holds us back from realizing our true potential. When it comes to currency trading, this statement might be even more evident. Despite what could be a yearning to keep currency trading within the confines of your traditional stock and bond account and the gravitational pull of what seems to be simpler math in currency ETFs relative to FX and futures, I'd like to challenge your perception. Perhaps thinking outside of the box will open the door to efficiency and hopefully profitable speculation.

As you should be well aware by now, both the futures and FX markets involve a substantial amount of leverage. As a result, each of these methods of speculation tends to be scrutinized and criticized by those unfamiliar with (or, frankly, in the business of) selling equity products. However, substantial losses are possible in any market, and ultimately it is the trader who chooses the level of leverage she can, or should, take on. That said, it doesn't seem fair to blame the trading venue when the blame is likely more accurately pointed toward the participants themselves. The FX and futures markets clearly offer traders a heavy dose of negative temptations, such as overleveraging and overtrading, but there aren't any obligations to give in to them!

Before we can fully decipher whether or not ETFs are a viable choice for currency speculation, we must first cover a fundamental difference between trading leveraged markets such as FX and futures and trading equity market ETFs. As you've learned, contracts traded in the FOREX and futures markets are not assets; they are liabilities. Simply put, traders in the futures and FX markets are buying and selling obligations to make or take delivery of the underlying currency at a particular price and time in the future. This goes completely against the basis of the equity markets, where each participant believes he has purchased an "investment" in an asset that he trusts will gain in value over time. Therefore, unlike equities, futures and FX contracts have no sense of ownership.

I find the lack of owning a concrete asset has the ability to turn speculators away. For many, it feels more like gambling, or scalping NFL tickets, than investing. Nonetheless, the truth is that any venture into the currency markets would be a stretch to label as "investing." Currencies don't pay dividends and in the long run are nearly directionless. For the most part, currencies trade within a historical range filled with massive ups and downs, whereas traditional equities have historically traveled higher in the long run.

Also, let's face the facts: Currency market ETFs are often funds that hold futures contracts. So while your stock brokerage statement might classify holdings in such a fund as an asset, you are, in a roundabout way, trading the same obligations and liabilities that you are trying to avoid by dodging the futures and FX markets.

Convenience, along with the perception of simplicity and easy access, are compelling reasons to consider trading equity ETFs, but there are certainly arguments that favor ditching the comfortable for what might be more efficiency. I have already mentioned a few supporting factors of this premise, but let's take a closer look at the details.

High Annual Expense Ratios

Currency ETFs tend to have high annual expense ratios relative to other fund strategies. After all, you now know that financial futures contracts expire four times per year and therefore funds holding assets in the futures market must make sizable transactions at least quarterly. In addition, there will likely be some rebalancing going on simply because as market prices fluctuate so does the weighting of the fund; therefore, transaction costs could be pricey.

Tendency to Lure "Green Investors"

I was once told that being a broker is nothing more than being a "glorified salesman." I'd say that holds true for brokers as well as brokerage firms, and anyone else who makes a living packaging and marketing financial products. Those responsible for the advent of the simple stock index ETF and all the subsequent strategies and alternative asset ETFs are certainly seasoned salespeople.

They realize most traders will opt for products that are easily and conveniently accessible regardless of efficiency and logic. They also know that the average retail investor isn't necessarily in tune with the world of finance, but most of them believe that they are. Accordingly, they might be eager to nibble on ETF products that feature the current buzzwords of the financial press and television. For instance, in early 2011 the gold and silver ETFs (GLD and SLV) soared in popularity largely because the popular business news stations, Internet media, and newspapers were inundated with the precious metals story. At one point, there was more volume going through the SLV than there was the SPY (the original S&P 500 ETF)…and that is simply insane. Yet, the reasoning was simple: Anybody with a brokerage account and a computer (with a mouse attached, of course) could easily buy gold and silver ETFs with the click of a button. Not only does this add fuel to the frenzied fire, but it lures novice traders and investors into markets they really don't understand and probably shouldn't be dabbling in.

In the case of currency ETFs, it is feasible to assume that many investors don't realize these simply aren't buy-and-hold products. They are highly speculative directional trades that otherwise have little value.

Don't Be Fooled by ETNs

An ETN (Exchange Traded Note) is a senior, unsecured, unsubordinated debt security issued by an underwriting bank. Unlike ETFs, ETNs are not investments in a fund; instead, purchasers are acquiring debt from the issuer, which involves a maturity date. The issuer will pay a one-time payment based on the underlying currency but, of course, the value of the ETN fluctuates in the market to reflect performance, so don't get excited assuming there is no risk of loss.

Although they are far less popular than ETFs, currency ETNs are listed and available to retail investors. Unfortunately, many fail to conduct due diligence and unknowingly commit money to ETNs, subjecting themselves to default risk by the issuer. The odds of a default might not necessarily be substantial or even somewhat likely, but why take the chance? It seems as though most investors agree, ETNs across all assets and strategies have only attracted about 1% of the capital that ETFs have.

On the other hand, ETNs do offer favorable tax treatment over ETFs, but traders can enjoy similar, and perhaps even more attractive, tax efficiencies in the futures and FX markets.

The ETF Doesn't Always Follow the Underlying Currency

ETFs are essentially derivatives of a derivative, and for fund managers it can be a daunting task to structure the fund in a manner in which the payouts mimic the underlying asset. In the case of unleveraged and long funds, this is a less obstructive obstacle. However, for those who are attempting to trade double, triple, or more leverage or short currency funds, the actual results may vary widely from the changes in asset price. For instance, naive investors might assume that an X% move in the underlying currency would increase or decrease the value of their fund in the same increment, but this just isn't the case. As savvy and clever as the creators of these funds are, they simply cannot tell the future— which is what it would take to accurately balance and rebalance the fund before market values change. Accordingly, the funds are really able to follow the asset for only brief stints or a single trading session. In other words, "buy-and-holders" should look elsewhere for exposure to the currency markets.

Commission on Top of Fees!

Not only do currency ETFs have a tendency to rack up sizable internal trading costs, but those wishing to purchase shares of the fund also must pay commission to enter and exit the trade. Obviously, there are commission expenses for trading in the futures market, and those trading FX with an ECN broker will also pay a commission (don't forget that those with non-ECN brokers aren't getting off scot-free), but in the ETF format, traders are essentially covering the cost of the fund's commission as well as the ETF commission. Bluntly, they are paying transaction costs twice. Depending on rates or time horizon, this may or may not be a deal breaker, but it is certainly something to be aware of.

Free and Flexible Leverage

Futures and FX traders enjoy access to high levels of *free* leverage, but ETF traders face substantial fund management fees and, in many cases, brokerage margin interest fees to add leverage to their currency holdings. I'll admit that leverage is something that shouldn't be used in full force, but I find that a little bit of a good thing might go a long way, and unnecessarily paying for access to it simply gets in the way of profits. I argue that the cost of leverage in the equity markets shifts the odds of success away from traders and toward stock brokerage firms.

As a reminder, leverage in futures and FOREX is ultimately determined by the trader through various levels of account funding—not the characteristics of the market being traded.

Long or Short at the Click of a Button

Perhaps one of the biggest arguments against trading ETFs over FX and futures is the inability to quickly, easily, and efficiently go long or short any currency. ETF traders have the ability to purchase funds that profit when the currency in question rises, and to purchase funds that profit when the currency drops (known as **short** or **inverse funds**), but the logistics are slightly more complicated for ETFs. In the case of the short ETF, the trader isn't guaranteed that the fund will be able to keep up with the actual performance in the underlying currency. It is difficult enough to make money through aspects that traders can control, such as whether to buy or sell, when to do it, and in what quantity, but leaving the fate of your trade up to the mathematics of constant rebalancing on the index seems to be an unnecessary complication.

On the flip side, stock brokers might be willing to loan shares of "long" ETFs to traders to enter as a short sale. However, they are subjected to the uptick rule and involve interest charges that work against the profitability of the trade...not to mention interest charges.

Cheap Market Access

Futures and FOREX traders are accustomed to the idea that it is possible to open a trading account with as little as $1,000, or in some cases even lower, and try their hand at currency speculation. However, this is not a possibility for those seeking to trade currency ETFs. Brokerage firms would likely not approve leverage on such an account size, and the purchase or sale of nonleveraged currency ETFs with limited funds creates a difficult environment for traders to come out ahead of the game. On the contrary, they probably don't have much at risk either. For instance, it would be possible to purchase seven shares of the FXE at a price of $140.06 within the confines of a $1,000 account while leaving some room for commission. Assuming a purchase price of seven shares at $980.42 ($140.06 per share), it would take a relatively large move in the underlying currency to recoup the commission paid, let alone make the venture worthwhile. If the Euro rallied 10 cents against the Dollar, the FXE should be valued at $150.06, yielding a profit of $10 per share, or $70 for seven shares. Assuming a commission rate of $10, which in stock trading means another $10 upon exiting the trade, the net gain would be a mere $50. Even a low margined E-micro futures contract would have gained $1,250 before commissions and exchange fees. Of course, with reward comes risk—the E-micro futures traders would have lost $1,250 on a drop in the Euro by the same amount. Nevertheless, the point is that currencies tend to trade sideways in the long term, and therefore traders would either have to dedicate massive amounts of capital toward the speculation to give themselves a chance to make money or they would have to work with leveraged ETFs or use the leverage granted by their brokerage firm. Much of the hassles and obstacles described here can easily be avoided by using the futures and FX markets.

Favorable Tax Treatment and Ease of Reporting

In regard to taxes and tax reporting to the IRS, futures and FX traders tend to feel sorry for stock traders. I'm not talking about the buy-and-hold investors, but rather those who are actively trading and speculating in the stock market. The reasoning is two-fold: For one, FOREX and futures traders are only required to report a single profit-and-loss figure, as well as the net of all fees, to the IRS. This is in contrast to the line-by-line reporting in equities that oblige traders to report the profit and loss for each individual trade. As you can imagine, this could be a potentially cumbersome, time-consuming, and error-prone task for active traders.

Here is the nail in the coffin in regard to the equity argument. Futures and FX traders, assuming they are speculating profitably, face much less of a tax burden than do stock and ETF traders. In futures and FX, there is no distinction between long-term and short-term capital gains. Instead, all trades are taxed at a 40%/60% blend between long and short term. This is significant because long-term gains are taxed at a lower rate than short-term gains. Even the profit on a trade that has a time span of a minute will be taxed 40% at the preferable long-term gains rate. This is, of course, presuming that at the end of the year the cumulative results are positive.

The Bottom Line

Although correctly predicting currency price changes and efficient execution of those ideas are the most important factors determining trading success, choosing the optimal currency product and brokerage firm comes in at a close second. For instance, the additional transaction costs, counter-party risk, and conflict of interest that comes with opening an account with a dealing-desk FOREX brokerage can have a profoundly negative impact on trading results for obvious reasons. However, there are less than obvious consequences as well, such as the psychological impact on trading decisions stemming from frustrations and mistrust of your broker. Hopefully I've armed you with the understanding of the pro's and con's of each trading venue to enable you to make an educated decisions based on your circumstances. Table 8-2 provides a side-by-side comparison depicting my opinion of the trader experience in all three arenas—FOREX (both dealing-desk and ECN brokers), futures, and ETFs—with five stars being most favorable and one star being least favorable.

Table 8-2   Side-by-Side Comparison of All Three Trading Arenas

	FOREX	Futures	ETFs
Margin	****	***	**
Day Trading Margin	*	*****	**
Transaction Costs	**** (ECN) **(DD)	****	**
Liquidity	***** (ECN) ** (DD)	****	***
Market Hours	*****	****	**
Regulation	**	*****	*****
Broker Conflict	***** (DD) ** (ECN)	None	None
Counterparty Risk	*	*****	*****

9

Order Types and Choosing a Currency Trading Platform

T here is more to profitable currency trading than correctly speculating on the direction of price movement. In fact, I often remind beginning traders of the tremendous difference between being right and making money in the markets. For instance, if traders aren't prepared to properly act on their research and intuition, it is easy to let an opportunity pass them by. For this reason, it is imperative that you completely understand the mechanics, logistics, and terminology involved in executing your ideas. Unfortunately, I've witnessed too many novice traders make the fatal mistake of not being completely familiar with the trading platform and software they are using to enter orders—or even worse, not being able to decipher between order types quick enough to prevent devastation in their account.

The bottom line is that being prepared to act is just as important as knowing when to buy or sell. Misunderstanding order types and platform mechanics can be an extremely expensive and an unnecessary lesson to learn. As a broker, I tend to recommend traders (particularly those who didn't grow up using computers) place orders with a full-service broker over the phone until they are comfortable tackling the task on their own. A broker worth her weight in salt will not only provide seamless execution, but she will help the trader understand the platform and the tools available for execution while she is at it.

Order Types

Prior to electronic trading platforms, currency futures trades were executed in open outcry pits via hand signals and shouting on the floor of the CME. During that era, there were several order types that have now become obsolete thanks to the new computerized trading environments. Therefore, we are only going to discuss the most commonly used order types, but keep in mind that many currency-trading platforms enable traders to plot entire trading "strategies" in which multiple order types are arranged at specific intervals and are tied to the entry and exit of a single trade. After you're familiar with each type individually, we discuss how they might be used together to accomplish a common goal.

Market Order

The most convenient and commonly used order type is what is known as a **market order.** Such an order instructs the brokerage firm to execute a trade at the best possible price at that particular time. Keeping in mind that we know the bid is the best possible price at which a trader can sell, and the ask is the best price at which one can buy, it is easy to see that a market order is simply paying the ask or selling the bid.

A market order guarantees that you will receive a fill, but it doesn't guarantee that you will be happy with the price. Sometimes the best possible price at the time of the order isn't the best price for your trading account. Beware of currency pairs with low volume and large bid/ask spreads, such as many of the exotic FX products. Illiquid markets could mean that the best possible price, and therefore the fill returned on a market order, is an unfortunate one. Once again, I don't recommend actively trading in markets that aren't capable of providing the liquidity necessary for seamless entry and exit.

Placing market orders provides little control over the fill price, but it does give traders precise control over the timing of execution. Compliments of the electronic execution enjoyed by currency futures traders, ECN FX traders, and to a lesser extent dealing-desk FX traders, fills are instantaneous.

When to Use a Market Order

You might hear financial market gurus such as CNBC's Jim Cramer insist that you should never use a market order. However, what they are getting at is that if you are happy with entering a trade at the current market price, you should place an order to sell at the bid price or buy at the ask. This is essentially a market order, but it eliminates the possibility of blindly falling into the abyss of a massive market move such as the infamous flash crash that took place on May 6th of 2010 in the equity markets.

Market orders are incredibly useful in situations where time is of the essence. In such a scenario, the trader might value ensuring the order is filled over stipulating a slightly better fill price. Simply put, if your analysis and conviction suggest that missing the trade altogether is out of the question, a market order is appropriate.

Once again, when trading illiquid currency pairs or currency futures in which the spread between the bid and the ask are wide, market orders should *not* be used.

Limit Order

A **limit order** is a request to initiate a trade at a specified price or better; simply put, a limit order is one in which execution is only permissible if it can be done at a price set by the trader, or at an even more favorable price. Accordingly, you might hear this order type referred to as an "or better" order. Naturally, what is better for buyers is different from what is better for sellers; as a buyer you would be better off with a lower price, and as a seller you would be better off with a higher price. This is not unlike anything else in business, or life for that matter. Therefore, if you look at this concept logically, it will quickly sink in. For instance, if you are a storeowner, you list the price of an item because you want customers to pay that much or more for the product and you aren't willing to accept less. You are probably thinking that it would be rare for a customer to be willing to pay more than the listed price, and it is no different in the financial markets. Limit orders are typically not filled at a better price than is asked, but the trader is guaranteed that it will at least be filled at the noted price.

"For investors as a whole, returns decrease as motion increases."
—Warren Buffet

On the contrary, some buyers enter retail stores with a price point at which they are unwilling to compromise. Essentially, they are looking to purchase an item at a specific price or less; otherwise, they will opt to forgo the purchase. This is identical to the process of buying a currency on a limit order. The trader stipulates a price at which he would be willing to accept the position, or better.

Thus far, we have ignored a very important point in regard to an "or better" order. Contrary to what many assume, if the market reaches your price but never surpasses it, you are not necessarily owed a fill. If this happens, you might or might not receive a fill. This is because the bid/ask spread typically prevents a sell order from being filled at the limit price without the market trading beyond it. In other words, it has to "go through it to do it."

When to Use a Limit Order

Limit orders are most useful to currency futures and FX traders who are looking to buy at a much lower price than the current market, or sell at a much higher price than is possible at the moment. I recommend that traders use limit orders as profit targets, or as entry prices if they are looking for the market to travel a significant distance from the current price before they are willing to enter. It is always appropriate to use a limit order in a market with considerably wide bid/ask spreads.

I believe that the use of limit orders to attempt to nickel and dime the market on the way in and out will give you more heartache and grief than joy. Unless your strategy is to scalp a few pips at a time with a large quantity of contracts, getting greedy with the entry and exit price probably won't pay off. For instance, if a trader truly wants to be long or short a market, saving a pip on the way in probably won't have a profound impact on the overall outcome—but missing the trade altogether might!

Although I don't necessarily advocate futures and FX traders attempting to shave a tick off their fill price with limit orders, option traders *must* use limit orders. Doing so mitigates the impact of bid/ask spreads that are customarily much larger in the options market than in the spot FX and futures markets. Accordingly, a practice known as **splitting the bid** is common. When a trader splits the bid, he is placing a limit order at a price between the bid and the ask, hoping that the market maker will budge in his price and fill the order; in many cases, he will.

Stop Order (AKA Stop Loss)

A **stop order,** often referred to as a "stop loss" or simply a "stop," is an order to execute a contract at the market price once a specified price is reached. This may mean that the market trades at the stop price or the price falls within the bid/ask spread, at which time the ticket essentially becomes a market order.

I find that many beginning traders are more comfortable with the concept of stop orders relative to limit orders. This is probably because this type of order is used by many traders as a risk management tool—or, more specifically, to "stop" the pain of a trade gone bad. In most cases, stop orders are used to defend open positions from losses beyond the stated point or simply an attempt to lock in profits up to the stipulated price. Despite what most believe to be true, a stop order can be placed as a means of either entering or exiting a position. Some traders use stop orders to enter a market based on a perceived breakout of a trendline or trading range; the assumption of such a strategy is that if a market penetrates well-known support or resistance, it will likely continue in the same direction to yield a profit to those working stop orders beyond technical barriers.

A stop loss order is used with the opposite intentions of a limit order. Traders buying or selling on a limit are expecting the price to become more favorable before being due a fill; a stop order, on the other hand, requires that a market price become unfavorable before the trade is executed. In other words, a buy stop order would be placed at a price that is above the current market price, and a sell stop order should be placed below the current market price. As you can see, the buyer of a contract on a stop order will only be filled if the price goes up (unfavorable) and the seller of a contract on a stop will only be filled if the market goes down (unfavorable).

Also in contrast to limit orders, stop orders become market orders when the listed price is reached, so there is the possibility of undesirable slippage on the fill. Simply put, your actual fill price might differ from the stop price you had originally stipulated. In theory, the slippage may be favorable or unfavorable, but throughout my experience I have found that stop order slippage almost always works against the retail trader.

When to Use a Stop Order

Many traders rely on stop orders to eliminate the mental anguish of manually exiting a trade at a loss, or perhaps worse, offsetting a trade that was once a big winner at a price that is now much less. Imagine being long the EUR/USD FX pair from 1.3505, watching it rally to 1.3720 and then back down to 1.3400. Although the net result of the trade is a loss of 105 pips, the swing in account balance is equivalent to 320 pips (1.3720 – 1.3400), and this is exactly how your emotions will see it, too. Without a concrete stop order working, traders often have a hard time cutting a loss before it gets out of hand.

One Cancels the Other (OCO)

An **OCO order,** or a One Cancels the Other order, is referred to as a "contingency order" because it requires the broker (or your trading platform, if capable) to cancel one of your orders should the other be filled. An OCO order can consist of a combination of any order type, but most often involves a stop order and a limit order, or simply a profit target and a stop loss for a particular position. Many trading platforms offer the ability to set multiple stop and limit prices for multiple contracts traded. Therefore, they refer to OCO orders as "strategies" or "multiple exits."

When to Use an OCO Order

Before computerized trading, OCO orders were manually carried out by brokers on handheld tickets. As you can imagine, they were somewhat error prone and cumbersome. Luckily, today's traders are able to implement such a strategy with a few clicks of a mouse.

The convenience of modern-day electronically executed OCO orders makes trading more convenient and mitigates the possibility of erroneous fills occurring due to failure to cancel orders that traders no longer desire to be filled. For instance, traders who fail to use the OCO feature in their platform might have both a profit target (limit) order working simultaneous to a stop loss order. If one is filled and the other isn't properly canceled, it is possible both will be filled despite the trader's intentions.

GTC (Good 'Til Canceled)

Beginning traders often make the mistake of assuming all orders will continue to be active indefinitely, but that is not the case. Those intending their orders to continue to be in play must enter a Good 'Til Canceled order. Often called open orders, **Good 'Til Canceled (GTC) orders** are always considered active until filled, canceled, or replaced by another order. GTC orders can be any order type, but they are most often stop or limit orders.

When to Use a GTC Order

GTC orders are great in that they reduce the probability of error in trade placement simply because they directly reduce the number of conversations with your broker or the number of times you must enter the trade online if you are a self-directed trader. However, beginning traders have been known to place GTC orders and forget about them, only to find that disaster has struck while they weren't watching. If you are going to use GTC orders, make sure you properly monitor them, otherwise they might get filled when you least expect or desire them to.

Order Type Example

It is quite probable that a trader will use each of the order types mentioned within the same trade. In fact, most currency-trading platforms are capable of incorporating each at the onset of entering the position. Every platform differs in the manner in which such a strategy is entered and eventually executed, but a few examples are MEME (Multiple Entry Multiple Exit), Strategy Builder, and ATM Strategy (where ATM stands for "automated"). For the purposes of this text, we will simply refer to it as a "strategy."

A **strategy,** when correctly entered into a computerized trading platform, is a collection of user-defined rules that create and manage a set of entry and exit orders applicable to a trading position. It its simplest form, a strategy might be buying 100,000 worth of the EUR/USD at the market and immediately placing a stop loss at a predetermined distance from the entry price and a profit target (limit order) at a preset level. The strategy is intelligent and therefore knows the stop and the limit will be OCO orders. Thus, if one is filled, the other will be automatically canceled.

Most platforms with strategy capabilities require traders to enter the stop and limit orders in relative terms, such as the distance from the fill price, rather than at specific prices. Therefore, if a trade to go long the EUR/USD was filled at 1.4310 on the entry and the strategy called for a stop to be placed 50 pips beneath the fill price and a limit 100 pips above the fill price, the trader would have his stop at 1.4260 (1.4310 – 50) and his limit at 1.4410 (1.4310 + 100). Had the entry been at 1.4300, the stop would have automatically been placed at 1.4250 (1.4300 – 50) and the limit at 1.4400 (1.4300 + 100).

A more complex illustration of a platform strategy might be to buy 500,000 of the EUR/USD at the market (equivalent to five standard contracts) with instructions to place stop and limit orders at five various increments. Let's take a look at a specific example.

A trader who purchases 200,000 worth of the EUR/USD at 1.4500 might instruct his platform to place a stop order on 100,000 that is 30 pips below the entry price and a stop loss on the remaining 100,000 that is 50 pips below the entry price. Accordingly, his stop orders would be working at 1.4470 on half of his position and 1.4450 on the other half. In doing so, the trader limits his total risk on the trade to 80 pips, or $800 (each pip in the EUR/USD is always worth $10). Had the trader opted to place a limit order to exit the entire position 100 pips above the entry, or 1.4600, his profit potential on the trade would be $2,000 (100 × 2 standard contracts × $10). As mentioned earlier, when stop and limit orders are placed within the strategy window of a trading platform, they are typically automatically entered as OCO orders. However, they are generally not entered as GTC orders. It is up to the trader to denote whether the order will be GTC or simply a day order. Don't make the painful mistake of placing a stop order and a limit order and then walking away assuming they will work on a GTC basis when in reality they weren't set up that way. It might be a fun mistake to make if the market suddenly moves in your favor, above and beyond your intended profit target. Unfortunately, though, I've found that order entry errors rarely work in the favor of the trader…call it Murphy's Law.

Similarly, please don't assume that anytime you place a stop order and a limit order on the same contract that it will automatically be an OCO, because it won't. Again, each platform is different, and unless you are entering the stop and limit orders within the "strategy" window of your platform, they will likely be treated as completely separate orders. That said, most platforms have the capability of linking orders to make them OCO in case you entered the stop and the limit separately in an order entry window other than the "strategy." It is also important to realize that most platforms offer several ways to enter an order, and it is up to you to discover which will work best for your circumstances.

What You Need to Know About Currency Trading Platforms

Most FX and futures brokerage firms offer several trading platforms to their clients with various degrees of complexity, capabilities, and costs. In many cases, the trading platforms are completely customizable to the needs of each trader; accordingly, the choice between platforms can be daunting for a beginning trader. Although all traders must ultimately determine platform decisions, I hope to give you a few pointers to simplify the process.

In the end, it will be the trader and the trades that determine the fate of a currency speculation account. Nonetheless, a reliable and simple-to-use platform can avoid some of the unnecessary frustrations that come with inadequate trading software.

Prior to opening a trading account, it is a good idea to run a demo of a handful of trading platforms to get an idea of what you might or might not need. Although brokerage firms often offer at least one "free" trading platform, there will likely also be several paid for options. In this case, the term "free" is being used to describe the cost of the software you will be using to buy or sell currencies and not the commission, which is a separate transaction cost. Please note that, in FOREX, dealing desks typically offer platforms developed in-house (that is, by the brokerage itself); accordingly, they tend to have fewer platform options to choose from.

The cost of upgraded trading platforms vary widely; for instance, certain futures-trading platforms run into the hundreds (or even thousands, if there is built-in news and analysis) per month, whereas others cost under $50 per month.

In today's environment, nearly all trading platforms are integrated to offer order entry, real-time charting, and position monitoring all from the same screen. Whether or not paying for an upgraded platform is justifiable will depend on your account size, trading strategy, and volume. For instance, if you are trading mini FX contracts with a $1,000 account, it doesn't make sense to allocate $60 per month (more or less, depending on the platform) of your risk capital to pay for the use of a fancy platform. Similarly, if you are trading a $50,000 account but are executing position trades where you only make transactions once every several weeks, it also doesn't make sense to pay for platform features you won't be using. In general, if your strategy is more active and has a shorter time frame, you should expect your paid-for platform to be more helpful.

Many FX and futures platforms offer a built-in news feed. However, there are often several costly upgrades to the service offered. In my opinion, the more in-depth and detailed the news feed, the easier it is to get lost in the madness and quickly become overwhelmed. In such a scenario, traders can easily fall victim to "analysis paralysis," meaning they have a hard time pulling the trigger. They might second-guess their research due to a recently announced economic report. Even worse, they might chase markets higher or lower following an announcement, assuming that the reaction to the news will continue. Each of these scenarios can be a detriment to a trading account. I believe traders are better off taking the news for what it is: noise in a much bigger story.

FX Order Entry Pad

Whether you opt for currency trading in the futures, FX, or ETF market, you will likely be using an advanced trading platform in which orders can be placed quickly and efficiently. After all, brokerage firms make money on commission, and they want to make trading as much as possible, as easy as possible.

FX platforms are unique because they all have a trade pad, as shown in Figure 9-1. Various platforms have diverse versions of the trade pad, but from my experience, they all tend to have the same components. Because FOREX contracts are traded in increments of 10,000 (referred to as "minis")—or in the case of some non-ECN brokers, in increments of 1,000 (referred to as a "micro lot")—traders can easily adjust the size of their trade by toggling the currency quantity from a drop-down menu. Most platforms also have preset quantities, enabling traders to adjust size between commonly traded figures with a single click. In Figure 9-1, a trader wishing to trade 250,000 Euros would simply click the 250K button to toggle from the default size (10,000 in this figure) to 250,000.

Courtesy of PFGBEST's BEST Direct 8 Trading Platform.

Figure 9-1   A typical FX trading platform will have a quick order pad that enables traders to buy and sell with a single click.

Most FX trading pads drop the "big figure quote" and merely display the last two digits of the quote on actionable buttons for both the bid and the ask. The big figure quote is the stem of a rate, and in most instances FX traders are referring to the big figure as anything other than the last two digits of a market price. In an effort toward simplicity, the ask button is often green to denote "buy" and the bid button is red to signify "sell."

In Figure 9-1, the bid is 1.44156 and the ask is 1.44168 (displayed in the top corners of the trading pad); a trader wishing to buy at the market would simply click the button that displays the ask (in this case, the green 16). To sell at the market, the trader would simply click the button with the bid (in this case, 15). By clicking the 16 button, the trader is agreeing to purchase the default quantity (10,000, in this example) of

Euro at the market. Keep in mind that the bids and asks are constantly moving, and an order to buy at the ask is essentially a market order. If in the small chance the ask changes as you are clicking the button, you might end up paying slightly higher for your Euro. You might be wondering why the quote provided is 15 bid at 16, when the true bid is 1.44156 and 1.44168. This is because the last digit of each of these quotes is the fraction of a pip rather than the full pip. Traders using this platform are able to buy and sell pairs in tenths of a pip, rather than the traditional full pip.

If you are concerned about the fill price to the tenth of a pip, or if the potential for slippage in the fill bothers you, an alternative would be to use a limit order, which agrees to buy 10,000 Euro at a price specified by you, or better. With a limit order, there are no surprises on the price of your fill, but you do run the risk of not being filled if the counterparty isn't willing to take the other side of your trade at the price you are asking for. I find that many beginning traders find this to be frustrating; they somehow feel as though they are being slighted if they enter a limit order near the current bid or ask but don't get filled. In reality, participants build the financial markets on the premise of free choice, and this isn't any different from any other marketplace; you probably wouldn't go into the grocery store and demand to be able to purchase a loaf of bread a nickel under the asking price. The bottom line is, if you want to play, you will have to pay. Nobody is obligated to play with you; that is what makes a market.

Futures Trading DOM (Depth of Market)

In the world of equities, traders are able to view market depth through what is known as a "Level II panel," but in futures it is referred to as a "Depth of Market (DOM) panel" and less commonly known as an order book.

The **DOM panel** displays the size of volume available in a particular currency within several ticks above and below the current market price. Simply put, the DOM panel displays the number of limit orders working to buy a currency and the number of limit orders working to sell a currency at prices surrounding the current market value. DOM panel data is displayed in real time and is therefore constantly changing as traders enter and cancel orders. Keep in mind, the DOM displays limit orders placed by other traders and market makers but does not display stop orders or market orders. This makes sense because market orders are filled instantly and stop orders become market orders once the stated price is reached.

Futures-trading DOMs have qualities similar to the typical FX trading pad but tend to be displayed in a different format. In my opinion, FOREX brokers designed the FX trading pad in an attempt to take attention away from the complexity of trading FX pairs. It can't get any easier than clicking a big red button to sell and a big green button to buy; unfortunately, that is where the simplicity ends.

Futures brokers, on the other hand, have taken a slightly different approach. Although they have the same goal of facilitating efficient and frequent trading, they tend to focus on flash and functionality. A typical DOM platform includes one-click buttons for buying and selling, just as the FX trading pad does, but futures platforms take it a step further. Most DOM panels provide traders with their trading stats, such as net position, average price, open profit and loss, and total profit and loss, within the same viewing window. There are also buttons that flatten the position, or reverse the position.

DOM panels are sometimes offered in FX platforms as well; however, the data being shown is derived from a much different source and therefore will have significant differences in regard to the size of the limit orders working (contracts available) at each price. Because FX isn't traded on a centralized exchange, brokerage firms may or may not offer access to DOM panels for FX products. Whereas in futures, market data includes the buy and sell orders of *all market participants,* FX platforms only display working orders of *those trading within the same ECN network or within the dealing desk* operated by the brokerage firm. For those FOREX firms that do offer DOM panel trading when accessing an ECN market, it is likely they will see relatively large orders working in round numbers at each of the nearby prices. These represent the quantity of contracts available from liquidity providers to the ECN, such as banks and financial institutions, who are acting as market makers. DOM panels offered by dealing-desk brokers tend to involve single-digit bids and offers during what is supposed to be the liquid trading day. Size is typically in the single digits (five to ten lots at each price), but sometimes there are as many as 15 lots available at each price. This pales in comparison to the number of contracts offered in a futures DOM, which is typically in the double and triple digits, ranging from 40 to 150 (see Figure 9-2).

| 6EU11 | ◦a | Pos: | + 1 | Avg: | 1.4374 | Hi: | 1.4393 | Lo: | 1.4365 | Chg: | +0.0001 | OPL: ($12.50) | TPL: ($12.50) |

Flat MKT 6EU11	Rev MKT 6EU11
Buy MKT	Buy LMT	Sell LMT	Sell MKT
CXL Buys 6EU11	CXL All 6EU11	CXL Sells 6EU11

Trades	Volume	Offset P/L	▶	Bid Size	Bid	Ask	Ask Size	▶	Offset P/L	Volume	Trades
65	103	($12.50)		5	1.4373 (1)	1.4374	T		$0.00	150	61
44	54	($25.00)		55	1.4372	1.4375	6		$12.50	94	64
37	43	($37.50)		43	1.4371	1.4376	65		$25.00	114	85
42	50	($50.00)		61	1.4370	1.4377	56		$37.50	109	79
27	34	($62.50)		55	1.4369	1.4378	48		$50.00	76	61
23	27	($75.00)			1.4368	1.4379			$62.50	57	48
12	14	($87.50)			1.4367	1.4380			$75.00	46	38
10	12	($100.00)			1.4366	1.4381			$87.50	51	39
4	4	($112.50)			1.4365	1.4382			$100.00	29	18
		($125.00)			1.4364	1.4383			$112.50	49	36
		($137.50)			1.4363	1.4384			$125.00	70	50
		($150.00)			1.4362	1.4385			$137.50	65	45
		($162.50)			1.4361	1.4386			$150.00	27	20
		($175.00)			1.4360	1.4387			$162.50	62	51

Courtesy of QST futures trading software.

Figure 9-2   A typical currency futures trading DOM panel displays the number of contracts working at several prices above and below the current price and offers one-click solutions for buying, selling, reversing positions, or flattening positions.

Futures-trading DOM panels will vary in complexity and information, but the goal is to provide traders with fast and efficient access to primary trading functions. Most will display the open positions carried in the account for the currency in which the DOM is pulling data. Some of the more advanced DOM panels, such as that displayed in Figure 9-2, will show the OPL (Open Profit & Loss), TPL (Total Profit & Loss for that currency and trading session), the high, low, and last prices for the currency futures contract being traded—and they might even display the average entry price. The average price calculates the effective price the trader is long or short from, based on multiple entry levels. Nearly all DOM panels will have buttons to buy or sell the currency at the market as well as settings to control the number of contracts these buttons will execute.

Some DOMs offer limit order buttons, which will pull up an order ticket, prompting the trader to enter the price at which she would like to work the limit order. However, a better way to place a limit order in a DOM panel is to simply right- or left-click (depending on the settings of your DOM) on the price at which you would like to enter the order. For instance, some DOMs interpret a right-click on a price within the DOM as an order to sell at the clicked-on price and a left-click as an order to buy at the clicked-on price.

As you can see, DOM panels offer traders extremely quick order entry, but they do introduce a few potential issues. For one, the ease and control offered to undisciplined traders can easily encourage overactive trading, which has a tendency to work against the overall success of a trader. On the other side, those without a good grasp of computer use (and the ability to pay attention to the task) might be prone to expensive errors in placing unwanted trades or might enter their orders incorrectly. After all, if the difference between buying or selling lies in a right-click or a left-click, there is plenty of room for incorrect clicks in the heat of the moment.

Keep in mind, you will only be able to view and trade positions in the DOM in the currency product that is currently in view. In Figure 9-2, the trader has loaded the 6E (standard-sized Euro currency futures contract) into the DOM and therefore will only be able to trade and view Euro positions within the account in this trading DOM. However, by simply opening another DOM panel and loading an alternative currency symbol, he can trade that currency within that particular DOM. This might sound obvious, but it is somewhat common for beginning traders to click the Flatten button and assume the entire account is flat when in reality they are holding positions in other currencies (not all DOM panels are as descriptive as the one shown in Figure 9-2, which stipulates which contracts are being flattened).

Trading by Phone

Technology has brought the markets into the homes of many people who probably wouldn't otherwise speculate in currencies; nonetheless, software and Internet connections aren't infallible. It is critical that you choose a brokerage firm (or individual broker) that is equipped to accept FX and futures orders over the phone.

Believe me, if you trade long enough, there will eventually come a time when either your computer freezes, your Internet connection goes down, or your broker's platform or trading server experiences technical difficulties. I'm sure you can imagine the frustration and panic that accompanies such a scenario, and this will be magnified tremendously for those unable to exit their positions by calling their brokerage firm. Profitable trading is difficult during times in which you are able to control entry and exit timing, but being "stuck" in a trade is not only frustrating, it might be financially devastating.

Side-by-Side Trading

Many brokers offer access to both FOREX pairs and currency futures within a single trading platform. Because the two products are traded in completely separate environments and with differing regulations, such trading actually requires two separate accounts: one for FOREX and one for futures. However, once you are logged in to the trading platform, you will see your positions and balances between the two accounts combined; therefore, it seems as though you are trading both FX and futures from the same account.

Popular Currency-Trading Platforms

Among the most popular third-party currency-trading platforms are Trade Navigator, NinjaTrader, Strategy Runner, and MetaTrader. Each of these platforms is broker agnostic, meaning that the software development took place by an independent firm and can be used by traders at various brokerage firms, as opposed to a trading platform developed by the broker itself. Keep in mind, not all brokerage firms will offer all third-party platforms. If you find something you like, you had better make sure your proposed brokerage firm is compatible with the platform you are set on. Nevertheless, most firms that *don't* offer NinjaTrader, MetaTrader, or some other popular third-party platform *will* offer something very similar.

10

Currency Options

The mechanics of option trading, the theories of option analysis, and even execution of options trades can be somewhat complicated and extensive. Therefore, the goal of this chapter is to introduce the topic and to point out some of the advantages and disadvantages involved with trading currency options in the futures and FX markets. Although I don't have the means to give the subject of options strategies justice within this text, you should walk away from this chapter with the ability to make a sound venue decision based on your trading needs and comfort level.

Currency options provide a flexible and effective way to gain exposure to the foreign exchange markets with various amounts of potential risk and reward. Options can be bought or sold outright, in combination with underlying spot FX or currency futures positions, or even as a package in which long and short options of various strikes and types are held to achieve a common goal. For example, through the combination of long and short calls and puts, an investor can design a strategy that fits his needs and expectations—such an arrangement is referred to as an **option spread.** That said, at the time of this writing, I was unable to find an FX options broker that offered packaged spread trading similar to what can be found in futures. Spread traders in FX options must buy and sell each individual option to create the overall strategy, piece by piece.

Each trader must determine his appropriate option trading strategy based on personality, risk capital, time horizon, market sentiment, and risk aversion; I believe it to be a worthwhile venture to be fully educated on the various market approaches. Simply put, you owe it to yourself to do as much homework on the logistics of trading as you would probably do in price speculation.

As a side note, risk-averse traders should stay away from option strategies that could inflict a great amount of pain, even if it means lowering the profit potential. Doing so could work toward avoiding panic liquidation at inopportune times as well as other unsound emotional decisions.

Options Basics

For the scope of this text, we will stick to the basics of options simply because delving further into the topic would require more chapters. Without this basis, it is almost meaningless to discuss the differences between futures and FOREX options. In currency futures, there are really only two types of options; however, FOREX traders might tell you otherwise.

The two basic types of options are **call** options and **put** options, as detailed in the following list. Note that the buyer of an option pays a premium (payment) to the seller of an option for the right, not the obligation, to buy (call) or sell (put) of the underlying futures contract at a stated price (known as a strike price), at or before, a stipulated date and time. Clearly, the right is more valuable (higher option price) for strike prices that are closer to current market values and for options with more time to expiration. The act of taking delivery of the underlying currency at the strike price is known as **exercising**, which stems from the fact that such traders are choosing to exercise their right. This financial value is treated as an asset (albeit an eroding one) to the option buyer and a liability to the seller.

- **Call options**—Call options give the buyer the right, but not the obligation, to buy the underlying currency at the stated strike price within a specific period of time. Conversely, the seller of a call option is obligated to deliver a long position in the underlying futures contract from the strike price should the buyer opt to exercise the option. Essentially, this means that the seller would be forced to take a short position in the market upon expiration.

- **Put options**—Put options give the buyer the right, but not the obligation, to sell the underlying currency at the stated strike price within a specific period of time. The seller of a put option is obligated to deliver a short position from the strike price in the case that the buyer chooses to exercise the option. Keep in mind that delivering a short futures contract simply means being long from the strike price.

Not unlike any other market, there are two sides to every options trade: a buyer and a seller. Options buyers are paying for the underlying right to buy or sell a currency at a stated price, whereas sellers are selling that right and accepting the liability of something going adversely. You've probably heard, or read, that the advantage of options trading is the luxury of limited risk. However, this isn't always the case; the most important thing to remember is that options *buyers* are exposed to risk limited to the amount of premium paid, but options *sellers* face theoretically unlimited risk. Conversely, option buyers have the possibility of potentially unlimited gains, but the profit potential for sellers is limited to the amount of premium collected. Simply put, the risk and reward profiles for option buyers and sellers are the exact inverse of each other. Also, when dealing with option spreads in which there are multiple long and short options of various types, the risk may or may not be limited. If there are more long options of the same type (call or put) than short, the risk is limited. If there are more short options (of the same type), the risk of the spread is unlimited.

Traders who are willing to accept considerable amounts of risk can write (or sell) options, collecting the premium and taking advantage of the well-known belief that more options than not expire worthless. The premium collected by a seller is seen as a liability until the option is either offset (by buying it back) or it expires. Option selling is based on the same model that insurance companies operate; they know that they will eventually face large claims but hope that the premium collected in the meantime covers their risk and leaves room for profit.

Once again, option buyers face limited risk but option selling involves unlimited risk. Don't forget: Option buyers and sellers have the exact opposite intentions and risk/reward profiles. Therefore, buying calls and selling puts is a bullish strategy, but buying puts and selling calls is bearish, as shown in the following table.

	Call	Put	
Buy			Limited risk
Sell			Unlimited risk

Not All Options Are Created Equally

Although it is true that the mechanics of calls and puts will be reasonably alike across all trading arenas, the options traded in FOREX are vastly more diverse than the instruments traded in the futures markets, or even stocks for that matter. For instance, FX traders face much different competition than do currency futures traders and also have the ability to individually negotiate the terms of the options being traded.

Standardized Versus Negotiable

The primary difference between FX options and options written on currency futures is the fact that FOREX traders aren't necessarily trading standardized contracts. In the world of futures, options are traded on an exchange such as the Chicago Mercantile, and each option carries the same specifications in regard to expiration date and time, size, and terms. In other words, the only negotiable aspect of a particular futures option is price. This isn't necessarily the case in FOREX; FX traders are able to negotiate specific terms with their broker, such as expiration date, and perhaps even the time of day. However, for simplicity, brokerage trading platforms often provide traders with a default expiration date and time.

Because FX options are not standardized and can be individually negotiated, they are not traded on a formal exchange. Instead, FX option trades are executed on a synthetic market created by the brokerage firm you are trading with (that is, a dealing desk). Simply, the house is taking the other side of trades and acting as the market maker. Obviously, this eliminates the benefits of an exchange, such as tight regulations, transparency, liquidity, and exchange guarantees (no counterparty risk).

FX options-trading platforms typically have a button labeled "RFQ" (for Request For Quote). This is necessary because individually negotiated expiration times, dates, and so on, require individual pricing rather than natural market price discovery. The lack of transparency in FX options creates a challenge in that it can sometimes be difficult to determine whether traders are being presented with fair market prices. After all, FX option traders are at the mercy of their brokerage firm when it comes to the price at which they can buy or sell (don't forget, the FX broker is also the market maker).

Keep in mind that FX options are not necessarily a commonly offered product by FOREX brokers, and for the most part are only available through dealing-desk brokerage firms. This is because, as previously mentioned, the flexibility of choosing the specifics of an option can make it difficult for traders to determine a fair price for the security; even worse, they are trading against their brokerage firm and are required to accept their broker's valuation. Even if FX traders could determine a fair price of an individually negotiated option, there isn't any guarantee the broker will agree to take it. After all, we aren't talking about free and open markets in which there is proper price discovery via several bids and asks from various counterparties. Not surprising, many of the larger FX firms have stated that they see very little interest in option trading by their clients.

Unnecessary Counterparty Risk in FX Options

In addition to the lack of transparency provided to FOREX option traders, players must rely on their FX brokerage firm to make good on their trade. For instance, a trader who buys a EUR/USD call option and later sells it at a higher price will reap the benefit of that profit only if she successfully withdraws all the funds from her account. Until then, it is entirely possible (yet, perhaps not probable) that the brokerage firm could go insolvent, taking her profits down with it. This isn't a common occurrence, but it can and does happen. (Remember REFCO?) A futures trader, however, does not face the same challenges.

Spreads You Can "Drive a Truck Through"

Throughout this book we have discussed the implications of the bid and ask spread. Specifically, the wider the spread faced by traders, the larger the transaction costs will be and the larger the obstacle to making a profit. Keeping all these things in mind, the largest disadvantage I can see to trading FOREX options, rather than exchange traded options written on currency futures, is the size of the spread between the bid and ask prices.

An option written on a *futures* contract involves freely floating bids and asks that represent the best price a retail trader can buy (ask) or sell (bid). The bids and the asks are often provided by market makers (liquidity providers trading their own funds), but they might also be the working limit orders (buy or sell orders) of other retail traders. As a result of multiple market makers and retail traders competing in the same marketplace, the spreads between bids and asks are typically much more favorable (tighter) than would otherwise be the case.

FX option traders, on the other hand, are forced to pay the price their brokerage firm is willing to sell for (ask) or sell at the price they are willing to buy at (bid). As you can imagine, there is a lack of competition, and because the brokers stand to profit from client losses (for every buyer there is a seller, and for every winner there is a loser), they prefer to keep the odds in their favor. Accordingly, the standard spread between the bid and ask of an FX currency option is 10 pips, whereas traders of futures options typically pay anywhere from 1 to 4 ticks, but usually 2 or 3. To put this into perspective, 10 pips on 100,000 units of the EUR/USD currency pair in FX represents $100! Therefore, an FX trader is immediately losing this amount simply by entering the options market. Traders of futures options face a much more manageable hurdle.

In addition to higher transaction costs at the hand of a wide spread between the bid and ask prices, FOREX options could be a little more expensive relative to futures options. Because of differences in specifications, it is nearly impossible to compare these apples to oranges, but it is important to keep in mind that although prices on FX options can sometimes seem like a bargain relative to futures in Dollar terms, they are based on 100,000 units as opposed to 125,000 for most options on futures.

FX Options Are Exotic!

Although I've focused on the negative up to this point, there is a glaring advantage to trading options in the FX arena as opposed to currency futures—and that is exotic options. **Exotic options** are those that have unconventional characteristics; they are simply any option that is not a vanilla option. (For clarity, a **vanilla option** is the standard call and put that all of us are familiar with.)

I'm not necessarily convinced that exotic options are helpful in making profits, but I've always been an advocate of being aware of the possibilities. In certain situations, experienced and savvy traders might find the flexibility of exotic options useful. That said, exotic options traders probably aren't doing themselves any favors by participating in an options complex that could prove to be overwhelming for inexperienced traders. Additionally, the seemingly unlimited choices might easily lure traders into contracts that aren't in their best interest, but they sure are "interesting and fun."

To give you an idea of what I'm talking about, a popular exotic option is the **barrier**, which is where a specific price is set and if reached it will either "knock in" (enable) or "knock out" (disable) the option. In other words, the derivative will only be active if a certain event occurs, or in the case of a knock-out option will be inactive if a certain event occurs. Barrier options tend to be cheaper than vanilla options because they require more specific price movement and are, therefore, less likely to pay off. Obviously, this is a brief example that likely leaves you unsatisfied on the complexities of this type of exotic option, as well as others. However, my intention of introducing you to the concept of a barrier is to merely give you an idea of the complex nature of such instruments.

SPOT Options

Some FX brokers offer traders the ability to trade what are known as **SPOT options,** or Single Payment Option Trading. In SPOT options trading, the trader inputs a scenario (for instance, the USD/JPY will break 73.00 in ten days) and the broker provides a quote on the cost of the option. If implemented and the scenario takes place, the brokerage firm will convert the SPOT to cash.

The primary advantage in trading SPOT options is the simplicity of knowing that if your stipulated event occurs, you make money; otherwise, you lose the premium paid. Also, SPOT options enable traders to choose specific details of what they think might happen. However, SPOT options tend to be more expensive than traditional vanilla options and can be difficult to determine a true value for. Once again, FX traders must rely on their broker to offer a fair price. Additionally, SPOT options cannot be bought and sold before expiration like other options can. If you enter the trade and change your mind, it is already too late—you are forced to let your bet ride and let fate determine the outcome.

The Bottom Line

In conclusion, if you would like to speculate on currency valuations with options, I believe the best choice is the currency futures options traded on the Chicago Mercantile Exchange or even U.S. Dollar Index options traded on the ICE exchange. Although the CME does not offer traders the array of exotic options that the world of FOREX does, doing so provides traders the luxury of knowing they are participating in a transparent, regulated, liquid, and level playing field as opposed to being at the mercy of their broker, who is also their competition.

11

Currency Market Fundamental

There are essentially three basic forms of currency market analysis: fundamental, technical, and seasonal. You are likely familiar with the former two, but the third might come as a bit of a surprise. In actuality, seasonal analysis is normally lumped into the category of fundamental analysis. However, because it is often overlooked and can play such an important role in the financial markets, I believe it is worthwhile to refer to it separately.

> "Rule No. 1: Never lose money; Rule No. 2: Don't forget rule No. 1."
> —Warren Buffet

It would be nearly impossible to do these forms of analysis justice within the scope of this text; instead, my intention is to make sure readers are able to grasp the overall concepts of each method and to point out some of the common hazards traders fall into.

Currency Fundamental Analysis

The currency markets are highly complex in that market participants, and their motives for buying or selling, are vast and nearly infinite. Accordingly, making short-term, or even intermediate-term, speculative decisions based on market fundamentals can be a difficult task. Additionally, despite what logic might suggest, market prices are often driven by emotions, fear, and greed rather than what many analysts believe to be fundamentally probable.

The traditional definition of fundamental analysis is the study of the core underlying elements that influence the economies backing each currency. Specifically, fundamental analysts attempt to predict future price action through the study of areas such as interest rates, government policies, business cycles, and economic growth. However, I'd also like to introduce a couple areas of fundamental study that often get overlooked: market sentiment and "overcrowded" trades.

Fundamental Theories (AKA Supply and Demand)

Because of the massive nature of data involved in fundamental analysis, the practice can be overwhelming. Regardless of the time dedicated to deciphering the market's fundamental code, it can be extremely difficult to succeed without the help of other types of market analysis. Nonetheless, it is important that you understand the basic ideas of fundamentalists; even though you might not be making all your decisions based on this type of information, others might be. As a trader, you are competing against all other market participants, and it is crucial that you know who you are up against, what they might be thinking, and, more importantly, what might be motivating their actions.

Fundamental analysts attempt to simplify markets into a function of supply and demand; in fact, this is the basis for all fundamental premises. In theory, supply (currency to be sold) and demand (currency to be bought) can be quantified and used to predict, or at least explain, price movement. The basic concept is simple: All else being equal, an increased supply of a currency results in cheaper prices, and vice versa. On the other hand, an increase in demand for a currency will inflate the value.

However, in real life, "all else being equal" doesn't exist. As supply is changing, so is demand, and the simplistic two-lined diagram used to explain the relationship between the two might as well be twisted into a pretzel. For instance, to determine true supply and demand, an analyst would first have to decipher all the economic, social, and political forces that drive supply and demand...and that is no easy task.

Let's take a brief (and perhaps overly simplistic) look at a handful of traditional schools of thought that FX traders will continually be exposed to and that some use to attempt to predict price movement.

Interest Rates

As a reminder, currency traders are exposed to both interest rate and currency risk along with currency valuations. FOREX traders are directly affected by the interest rates backing each currency through daily rollover charges. Remember, if a trader is long the currency in the pair with a higher interest rate, he receives the interest rate differential, but if he is short the currency with the higher rate, he will pay interest each day. The impact to futures traders isn't as obvious, but because currency values are driven by corresponding interest rates, they are exposed to the same interest rate risk. For instance, a currency backed by a higher relative interest rate is more attractive; therefore, demand for that currency, with all else being equal, will be higher. Naturally, higher demand promotes higher prices.

> The market is never wrong.

With this in mind, it comes as no surprise that FX and currency futures traders are often keen on the relative interest rates behind the currencies they are placing wagers on. In theory, when a country raises interest rates, its currency strengthens relative to others, and vice versa. Of course, trading isn't quite this simple. Markets often "price in" changes in interest rates before they are actually put into effect. Simply put, markets are forward looking, and if the Fed, the ECB (European Central Bank), or any other central bank telegraphs its next move, the market is quick to react. Don't think that on the day of a Fed interest rate hike, making money in FOREX will be as simple as buying the USD/JPY or selling the EUR/USD. Nonetheless, you must be aware of the conventional wisdom that other market participants might be operating on.

Inflation/Monetary Policy

Inflation is an overall increase in the cost of goods and services that can be consumed within any given economy. During times of inflation, each unit of currency can buy fewer goods and services. Accordingly, inflation can best be described as erosion in the purchasing power of money. Simply put, a $1 bill will always be worth one Dollar, but as inflation takes hold, that single bill of currency will be able to buy less and less.

A full discussion of monetary policy, inflation, and thus currency valuation could span the length of an entire book on its own, so I'll keep it brief and simple. Economists like to describe the act of inflation as the result of too many Dollars chasing the same number of goods. Accordingly, consensus is that inflation is caused by excessive growth of the money supply, and currency markets tend to view this as a weakness in the associated currency value.

Ideally, traders would like to see currencies backed by low or moderate rates of inflation because such levels of price pressure can typically be attributed to real demand for goods and services or changes in supply of those goods and services, and not necessarily increases in money supply.

Central banks are responsible for manipulating inflation to desired levels through monetary policy. Monetary policy is the process of "controlling" a country's money supply to promote what are deemed favorable interest rates and inflationary pressures provided the current economic environment. In its simplest form, monetary policy is either expansionary or contractionary. **Expansionary policy** increases the money supply, lowers interest rates, and weakens the domestic currency. This practice is common during times of recession or high employment. **Contractionary policy,** on the other hand, results in a decrease in money supply, higher interest rates, and higher currency valuations.

The Fed provided a spectacular example of expansionary policy in the late 2000s by dramatically increasing the money supply and suppressing the value of the greenback to historically low levels.

Trade Balance

Concisely, the trade balance provides a quantitative snapshot of nations' imports and exports, or, more importantly, the net difference between the two categories. In general, a country that is experiencing more imported goods and services than exported, is seen as having a weaker currency. This is because in order for a country to purchase goods to import, it must convert the domestic currency (assumed to be U.S. Dollars in this text) into currency in which the goods are priced. In other words, when U.S. consumers are purchasing goods made overseas, they are in essence contributing to a lower Dollar value because they are indirectly willing to sell the dollar to purchase alternative currencies needed to acquire the desired goods.

Although I believe anybody participating in the currency markets should understand this concept, I have serious doubts as to whether monitoring monthly stats on trade balances will offer traders any type of edge in their speculation. Not only does the data severely lag reality by the time it is released, even real-time information will simply tell you what has already happened and not necessarily what will happen in the future. A country running a large trade deficit (more imports than exports) this month might improve the situation in the next month, but by the time you are privy to the information, the currency sales and purchases have already occurred and are built into market pricing.

Intervention

Similar to the popular A&E television series, the term **intervention** is used to describe a scenario in which an involved, or uninvolved, party interferes with a situation in an attempt to alter, or hinder, the natural development of the circumstances. Specifically, in the foreign exchange markets, regulatory agencies or governments sometimes intervene in market pricing by directly coercing currency exchange rates.

Intervention to control price can be done indirectly through the manipulation of imports and exports, or directly by the purchase or sale of large amounts of currency by central banks in the open market. If this seems a bit unfair to those speculating in the markets, it is; nonetheless, there are other agendas at play, and in the overall scheme of things speculators are at the bottom of the importance totem pole when it comes to government behavior. Unfortunately, this is something that must be understood, and accepted, by anyone wishing to trade currencies in any arena.

One of the most consistent interventionists is Japan. In mid 2003, after a nearly 14-year period of deflation and economic anemia, the Japanese central bank essentially printed 35 trillion Yen to purchase about $320 billion in U.S. Dollars, which were then parked in government-backed Treasury securities. The move immediately weakened the Yen against the Dollar and is said to be a big part in improved exports from Japan, which eventually lifted the country out of its deflationary period.

More recently, in March of 2011, the Japanese central bank made a similar attempt to cap a rally in the Yen against the U.S. Dollar. This time, it was actually a group composed of seven of the world's most influential central banks that intervened in what are normally free-floating currency markets. The USD/JPY was trading at an all-time low near 76.00 (equivalent to an all-time high in the futures market, near 129.50). Because the astronomical Yen valuation threatened the ability of the Japanese economy to snap back from a March 11, 2011 earthquake, the G-7 coordinated an operation in which each of the participating nations sold large amounts of Yen at the open of their respective trading day, beginning with the BOJ (Bank of Japan).

GDP (Gross Domestic Product)

You are probably aware that the Gross Domestic Product (GDP) of a nation is the total market value of all goods and services produced domestically, including foreign businesses operating within domestic borders. In other words, it is based on geographical location rather than nationality. In essence, GDP indicates the rate at which an economy is growing or contracting. Generally, a higher GDP rating is considered favorable to the currency it is backed by. Once again, knowing and understanding this theory is necessary in determining market sentiment and psychology, but likely won't help you in executing profitable short-term FOREX trades.

Drawbacks of Traditional Fundamental Analysis

Although I would never suggest traders ignore market fundamentals, I do encourage that they take the "story of the day" with a grain of salt. Despite widespread use of fundamental analysis by currency traders, it is important to realize that economic news and events are typically "priced into" market values immediately. Simply put, most financial theory supports the premise that current market pricing already reflects *all* available and known fundamental information.

Frankly, it is extremely difficult to have an edge when it comes to fundamental information. After all, in theory, all market participants will have access to the same information at the same time. Therefore, selling a currency pair

> "You adapt, evolve, compete, or die."
> —Paul Tudor Jones

merely because recent governmental data has been weak in regard to the base currency isn't necessarily putting the odds in your favor; instead, you might be selling for reasons that are already accounted for in the market price. If so, it is highly probable that prices will move higher once you go short. Don't forget, most traders lose money in the markets; accordingly, profitable trading is most likely much more difficult than selling the Dollar following a weak non-farm payrolls report. Even those with quick fingers will find it difficult to be quicker than all, or at least most, other market participants to yield a profitable trade.

Unconventional Forms of Fundamental Analysis

The less discussed aspects of fundamental analysis, and perhaps the most useful, are the practices of identifying extreme prices and overcrowded trades. Each of these concepts is nearly synonymous and built upon the fact that for every buyer there is a seller, and therefore markets cannot go up or down "forever," although it can sometimes feel as though they do. Concisely, if most traders are long a particular currency futures, or currency pair, the only way for them to exit the position is to take delivery of the currency (which isn't probable or practical) or to sell an equal amount of the currency they are long.

In such an event, market prices are capable of swift countertrend moves regardless of surrounding news events or circumstances. Simply put, it is profit taking; traders usually begin exiting overheated markets with market orders, but the move can quickly begin to trigger standing stop loss orders, and this is where much of the damage can be done. Regardless of the manner in which traders are fleeing the overcrowded trade, the result of liquidation is a sharp countertrend move. Figure 11-1 provides an example of a market that quickly shifts from an overheated rally to becoming dramatically oversold; in both instances, prices snapped back with little mercy for complacent traders in its way. Here are a few tools that can be used to identify markets that might be susceptible to a trend reversal, or at least a correction.

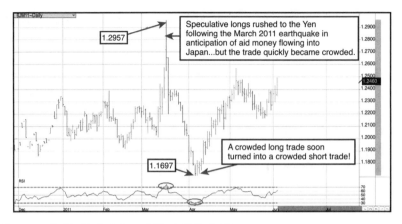

Charts provided by Gecko Software's Track N' Trade 5.0.

Figure 11-1   Markets often overshoot their "fair" price as traders blindly flock to the latest trade. Unfortunately, for the latecomers, irrational trend trading doesn't persist forever.

Identifying Market Extremes with High/Low Analysis

I've spent a considerable amount of time covering the academic concepts I believe to be necessary to build a base of currency market knowledge, so let's turn our focus to some of the less-talked-about, but perhaps more useful, components of currency market analysis.

Naturally, the most basic rule of trading is "buy low and sell high." Unfortunately, the concept is much easier to understand than to implement. Nonetheless, I tend to be on the constant search for markets that are trading at dramatic discounts, or premiums to the historical norm. There are no guarantees that markets trading at relatively expensive prices can't get even more expensive, or those at historically low prices can't get even cheaper, but probabilities suggest they likely won't.

Determining whether a currency is attractive based on past valuation can be done by simply viewing a long-term chart. Begin with a daily chart (meaning each price bar within the chart represents one single trading day) to get an idea of current price action, but then use a weekly

> "The stock market is a no-called-strike game. You don't have to swing at everything—you can wait for your pitch. The problem when you're a money manager is that your fans keep yelling, 'Swing, you bum!'"
> —Warren Buffet

chart (weekly price bars) to identify over- or undervalued currencies. Finally, move to a monthly chart to get the *big* picture (several years or more). Perhaps an easier way to filter through the data is to find a data source that provides stats on annual and monthly highs and lows in each of the 31 most heavily traded currency pairs. One such service is offered free at www.barchart.com. The site displays the year-to-date high and low of each currency future and most FX pairs on the High/ Lows page; it also offers stats on alternative time frames, including 5-day, 1-month, 3-month, and 12-month.

On the site, traders are provided with the magnitude of deviation from the currency price to the annual high or low in a percentage format. Using a source such as this could save traders valuable chart-scanning time and effort; as you can imagine, this type of easy-to-access, organized, and, even better, *free* information can be a valuable tool in determining which markets are possibly attractive for countertrend traders.

For example, as shown in Figure 11-2, by mid-October 2010, the U.S. Dollar index futures contract had retraced nearly all the progress made earlier in the year. A trader interested in a bullish play on the greenback might have simplified the research process by visiting the futures year to date high/low page on Barchart.com.

Commodities, typically agricultural, have the propensity to double, triple, or more, in the span of a year, but the currency markets rarely (or maybe *never* is more accurate) experience that type of volatility. Instead, currencies have a tendency to trade within a moderate price range on a year-to-year basis. Accordingly, when you are determining where the extreme price moves (and therefore possible bargains) might be, it is important to be able to put things in context by taking a step back to look at the big picture.

In the world of currencies, if a pair has gained or lost about 10% of its value from its recent, or annual, high, this might be something that should be put on the "watch list." Similarly, a move of 15% to 20% might be a sign that the market is overextended and could be setting up for an attractive countertrend move. Obviously, like any other tool or indicator, a 15% move from high to low doesn't constitute a buy signal in itself, but it should be considered an important piece to the analysis puzzle. After all, currency pairs that have suffered or celebrated massive moves in a relatively short period of time are often vulnerable to profit taking. Therefore, traders might be best off looking for the possibility of a trend reversal, or at least a corrective countertrend move.

			YTD	YTD	YTD	YTD	
Name	Contract	Last	High	High %	Low	Low %	Links
U.S. Dollar Index	DXZ10 (Dec '10)	78.377s	89.115	-12.05%	75.850	+3.33%	
British Pound	B6Z10 (Dec '10)	1.5771	1.6315		1.4313		
British Pound	B6H11 (Mar '11)	1.5757	1.6298		1.4324		
Canadian Dollar	D6Z10 (Dec '10)	0.97160	1.00160	-3.00%	0.92300	+5.27%	
Canadian Dollar	D6H11 (Mar '11)	0.96770s	0.99910	-3.14%	0.92790	+4.29%	
Japanese Yen	J6Z10 (Dec '10)	1.22420	1.24420	-1.62%	1.05610	+15.91%	
Japanese Yen	J6H11 (Mar '11)	1.22620	1.24530	-1.57%	1.06100	+15.52%	
Swiss Franc	S6Z10 (Dec '10)	1.01030	1.05720	-4.42%	0.86510	+16.81%	
Swiss Franc	S6H11 (Mar '11)	1.00950s	1.05740	-4.53%	0.86840	+16.25%	
Euro FX	E6Z10 (Dec '10)	1.37700	1.44930	-5.00%	1.19220	+15.48%	
Euro FX	E6H11 (Mar '11)	1.37450	1.44820	-5.08%	1.19300	+15.23%	
Australian Dollar	A6Z10 (Dec '10)	0.96720	0.99360	-2.64%	0.79500	+21.69%	
Australian Dollar	A6H11 (Mar '11)	0.95380s	0.98200	-2.87%	0.78890	+20.90%	
Mexican Peso	M6Z10 (Dec '10)	0.080050	0.081225	-1.60%	0.072825	+9.75%	
Mexican Peso	M6H11 (Mar '11)	0.079300s	0.080250	-1.18%	0.071875	+10.33%	
New Zealand Dollar	N6Z10 (Dec '10)	0.74010s	0.76080	-2.72%	0.65110	+13.67%	
New Zealand Dollar	N6H11 (Mar '11)	0.73450s	0.75250	-2.39%	0.64600	+13.70%	
South African Rand	T6Z10 (Dec '10)	0.140550s	0.145675	-3.52%	0.121275	+15.89%	
South African Rand	T6H11 (Mar '11)	0.138650s	0.143675	-3.50%	0.119425	+16.10%	
Brazilian Real	L6Z10 (Dec '10)	0.57810s	0.60100	-3.81%	0.49235	+17.42%	

Full List | Currencies | Energies | Financials | Grains | Indices | Meats | Metals | Softs

Currencies ⓘ HELP — Main View » Technical » Performance » Custom View

Courtesy of Barchart.com.

Figure 11-2 This snapshot points out that the U.S. Dollar index is down over 12% year-to-date and only 3.3% off the current year's low. Knowing currencies tend to trade in long-term ranges, traders might be best off cautiously favoring bullish positions.

An intra-day trader can also use the practice of looking for extreme moves; it isn't solely for the benefit of position traders. The difference simply lies in the price bars chosen; whereas day traders might focus on 15-minute bars, position traders might be looking at daily or weekly price changes. Of course, the length of the move also plays a big role in deciding whether the market might have gone too far too fast. Sometimes, orderly and slow-paced moves can extend well beyond the wildest expectations. Conversely, massive price changes in a short period of time often suggest trade is emotional and not fundamental.

Not only does scanning the markets for what are deemed extreme highs or lows determine where there might be attractive buying or selling opportunities, but it also provides some insight into the overall risk. Naturally, just because a futures contract is trading at, or near,

> Perhaps traders are best off doing the opposite of what is comfortable...buy the dips and sell the rips!

the "cheapest" level all year doesn't mean it can't get cheaper. Likewise, there is nothing that says it can't dip dramatically below the year-to-date lows, Nonetheless, this provides a sense of the big picture, enabling traders to determine whether the risk (based on history) justifies the potential reward.

Identifying Overcrowded Markets with the Commitments of Traders Report

If a stock trader wants to know what corporate insiders are doing with their shares, she looks to Securities and Exchange Commission (SEC) filings for help. Corporate officers, directors, and beneficiary owners are required to report trades they have executed in shares of their company within two business days. Similarly, a commodity trader looks to the Commitments of Traders (COT) report for insight into who is buying and selling futures and options. You might have noticed I used the term "commodity trader" rather than currency trader. This is because COT data compiled by the Commodity Futures Trading Commission (CFTC) is derived from futures markets stats only. Because FOREX is not traded on an individual exchange, it is impossible to collect the proper data needed to determine the net positions of FX currency traders. This makes perfect sense—not only are there several different ECNs in which FX is traded, but a plethora of dealing desks around the world execute currency trades for clients. Nonetheless, FX traders often use the COT report despite the fact that it reflects products traded on a completely different network. The information provided will likely reflect what is occurring in the FX markets; futures activity might not be a perfect representation of FOREX, but beggars can't be choosers.

The CFTC releases a weekly snapshot of the open interest on most futures contracts listed on U.S. exchanges. **Open interest** is simply the number of futures contracts that are held overnight (beyond the close of the day session) on the date in question; accordingly, open interest data does not include day trades in which positions are entered and offset within a single trading session.

The weekly CFTC report on open interest in the futures markets is referred to as the Commitments of Traders (COT) report, and it reveals a wealth of information on who is trading what and in which direction. More importantly, COT data provides a glimpse into the minds of other traders by depicting whether or not certain types of traders are bullish or bearish overall.

COT reports are available to the public free of charge via the CFTC's website (http://cftc.gov/MarketReports/CommitmentsofTraders/index. htm); it is even possible to register to have the information emailed directly to an inbox on a weekly basis. COT data sent directly from the CFTC arrives in plain-text format, and not unlike most government documents, it is much more difficult to decipher than it could be (see Figure 11-3). Fortunately, there are services that offer better organized and displayed information (see Figure 11-4).

```
CANADIAN DOLLAR - CHICAGO MERCANTILE EXCHANGE                    Code-090741
FUTURES ONLY POSITIONS AS OF 05/10/11                    |
-----------------------------------------------------------| NONREPORTABLE
        NON-COMMERCIAL      |     COMMERCIAL    |    TOTAL    |  POSITIONS
--------------------------|-------------------|-------------|--------------------
  LONG  | SHORT |SPREADS |  LONG  | SHORT  |  LONG  | SHORT  |  LONG  | SHORT
-------------------------------------------------------------------------------
(CONTRACTS OF CAD 100,000)                        OPEN INTEREST:      121,478
COMMITMENTS
  42,698    5,495      154  30,104  99,527  72,956 105,176  48,522  16,302

CHANGES FROM 05/03/11 (CHANGE IN OPEN INTEREST:    -18,441)
  -17,165     -327     -46    -636 -18,811 -17,847 -19,184     -594     743

PERCENT OF OPEN INTEREST FOR EACH CATEGORY OF TRADERS
     35.1      4.5     0.1    24.8   81.9    60.1    86.6    39.9    13.4

NUMBER OF TRADERS IN EACH CATEGORY (TOTAL TRADERS:      84)
       38       10       2      26     23      65      34
```

Courtesy of CFTC.gov

Figure 11-3 COT reports provided directly from the CFTC are difficult to read.

Commitments of Traders Analysis - Futures Only

Futures Only - 7/19/2011 - 7/26/2011						
	Non-Commerical		Commercial		Non-Reportable	
	Net Position	Weekly Net Change	Net Position	Weekly Net Change	Net Position	Weekly Net Change
Currencies						
Canadian	36,141	+8,377	-65,886	-9,202	29,745	+825
Dollar	2,328	-6,864	-4,738	+8,422	2,410	-1,558
Euro	17,038	+7,792	-25,744	-19,256	8,706	+11,466

Courtesy of The Hightower Report.

Figure 11-4 Services such as The Hightower Report offer easy-to-read interpretations of the CFTC's COT report.

Reading the COT report can be somewhat challenging, but it could be worth the effort. Reports are issued each Friday near the close of trading but are based on information measured on the close of business on the previous Tuesday. In other words, the report collects market data on Tuesday evening, compiles it, and makes it available to the public on Friday afternoon.

The purpose of the COT report is to provide information on market sentiment in a quantifiable manner. However, unlike a traditional sentiment index based on opinion polls, this measure only accounts for those who have actually put their money where their mouth is. Multiple versions are available, but in its simplest form, the CFTC determines the net position (long open interest minus short option interest) in three major categories: Commercials, Reportables, and Non-Reportables. In plain English, this translates into hedgers, large speculators (often called the "smart money"), and small speculators.

As an explanation, **reportable positions** are those held by single entities (individuals or funds) that exceed preset thresholds by the CFTC. For individuals holding positions in excess of the reportable limits, a daily tally is reported to the CFTC by the associated brokerage firm. The reportable limits vary by market and are typically very substantial. Most retail traders will not fall into this category; it is

> "Markets are constantly in a state of uncertainty and flux, and money is made by discounting the obvious and betting on the unexpected."
> —George Soros

often dominated by hedge funds, CPOs (Commodity Pool Operators), and CTAs (Commodity Trading Advisors) who are trading substantially large positions, and therefore account sizes. Conversely, **non-reportable positions** are those that don't meet the CFTC's reportable limits. Most, or perhaps all, of those reading this introductory book will fall into the category of Non-Reportable. The Commercials category represents end users or producers of the underlying asset and their established positions are for hedging purposes only. An example would be a firm that faces exchange rate risk and hedges accordingly. To recap, the Reportable category represents large accounts (high-capital accounts with a large position size), the so-called "smart money." Non-Reportables is made up of the small speculators, casually referred to as "dumb money," and Commercials is composed of legitimate hedgers.

COT reports are available in two formats: long and short. The short format separates open interest based on the categories just described, but the long format includes information provided in the short format as well as displays holdings of the largest four or eight traders represented in each contract. You might also run across an alternative version that includes open interest in options as well. In this version, all options held are converted into net futures positions by determining whether the option is bullish or bearish and to what degree relative to a traditional futures contract. For instance, a trader who is long an at-the-money Euro call would mathematically be long 0.5 futures contracts because his position is expected to make or lose money at the pace of half of a futures contract. This assumption is based on a mathematical concept known as "option delta" and is perhaps a little beyond the topic at hand. In my opinion, beginning traders will be able to get all the information they need from the traditional short format of the COT Report.

> The COT is a unique form of gauging market sentiment because it measures where traders put their money, not their mouth.

A handful of services are available that make the lives of traders easier by displaying the CFTC's COT data in a user-friendly format. One such example is the popular commodity trading newsletter *The Hightower Report* (www.futures_research.com), which for an affordable monthly fee issues color coded (green for long, red for short) figures with clear and concise net change figures (refer to Figure 11-4).

Similarly, Barchart.com has successfully created a visual depiction of this information, enabling traders to make educated decisions in regard to market speculation with less of the number crunching and stress. Barchart.com's COT charts are available for free to all site visitors (Figures 11-5 and 11-6, later in this chapter, provide examples of these charts.)

In essence, the CFTC's Commitments of Traders report displays the net position of each of the three aforementioned categories of market participants by subtracting the number of short positions from the number of long positions to determine a net figure. This net figure reveals not only whether speculators and hedgers are long or short the market, but it tells us by how much.

I feel as though the best use of information revealed by the COT Report is determining whether a market is overheated, and therefore vulnerable to mass liquidation. This can be looked at in a similar manner as an oscillator, such as slow Stochastics or RSI, in that it might indicate overbought or oversold market conditions. A well-known quip states, "Once the last man buys, the market sells," and the COT offers a behind-the-scene glimpse into when and where that *might* be. In other words, traders might benefit from monitoring the net long and short positions of each category to identify which markets might have accumulated large speculative positions, or where speculative interest is beginning to bud.

Putting the COT Report to Use

Markets, and therefore prices, are highly emotional simply because they are the result of the cumulative actions and reactions to events, news, and price action. In turn, currencies are subject to highly irrational price movements before reverting to what might be a more reasonable price. These irrational prices can be long lived and are often referred to as "overcrowded trades." There isn't a shortage of examples of overcrowded trades that ended poorly; think the tech bubble in 1999, the real-estate bust in 2006, and commodities in 2008. Not surprisingly, the same "irrational exuberance" (as Alan Greenspan might say) occurs in the currency markets.

Years of observation have lead me to believe the ability to avoid and survive the wrath of overcrowded trades is one of the most critical factors determining success and failure. As Warren Buffet once said in a CNBC interview, "We don't want to make money on the bubble; we just want to survive it without losing our shirts!" At the time he was referring to runaway gold and silver markets as speculators poured money into hard assets thinking they were "safe havens." They later discovered the volatile reality of the metals markets.

> Good trading decisions are born from experience; unfortunately, experience comes from bad trading decisions.

This herd phenomenon occurs repeatedly in the currency markets in various scales of extremes. For instance, in the spring of 2011, the U.S.

Dollar had suffered massive losses against most other major currencies but in particular the Euro. Once the average "guy on the street" became comfortable with the idea of the weaker dollar, the trend had nearly exhausted itself. Those who entered the market in early May on the long side of the Euro based on fundamental research that suggested interest rate differentials and inflation were favorable over the greenback, quickly realized that fundamentals don't always drive market prices and, even if they do, they are priced in advance. Those with their eyes open might be able to combat their greedy hearts. There are obvious signs of overcrowded trades, such as overbought oscillators and overwhelmingly lopsided sentiment in blogs, chat rooms, and news services. However, perhaps the best place to determine whether prices have been stretched too far is a quick look at the CFTC's COT report.

> Buy it when they cry, and sell it when they yell!

Had they looked at the COT, they might have realized they had already missed the boat. Small speculators were piling onto the trade and large speculators were holding massive long positions in the Euro. Overcrowded trades such as this can see vicious corrections; after all, in order to exit open positions traders have to do the exact opposite of what they did to get in (sell the Euro and buy the USD).

They say a bull market doesn't make a genius, and there couldn't be a truer statement; as a leveraged FX or futures trader, it is imperative to remember that the trend is only your friend until it ends. Traders must never forget, markets with high levels of speculative activity such as currencies have a tendency to overshoot an equilibrium price only to, at some point, revert to the mean as traders liquidate positions. After all, if all the buyers are in, there is nobody left to buy, and at some point, the longs will look to liquidate (sell). If a trade is dramatically overcrowded, the reversal can be treacherous, and saving yourself from its wrath could determine whether you are in the black at the end of the year.

The Commercials category is composed of large corporations, small businesses, and even individuals who are close to the action and relatively knowledgeable in the currency markets. Because of this, beginning traders often assume that "commercials" are the smart money they should be following and, therefore, they are apt to make the mistake of tracking this group. However, although highly intelligent individuals likely make the futures market decisions for those in the Commercials category, their motives are much different from those of the other COT categories. Commercials establish positions in the futures markets as a means of hedging their price risk in the cash market. In other words, their goal isn't to predict where the market is going or even profit from trades held in the futures markets; instead, they are simply offsetting risk of positions held in the cash market (future obligations to exchange currency). Accordingly, you will find that commercials are often on the wrong side of a price move in the futures market (but on the right side in their business operations). The COT is capable of telling the market's story, but in the case of the Commercials category it only tells half the truth!

> An overcrowded trade is a mild form of a bubble in which the masses jump on a directional bandwagon to force prices to extremes that might not have normally been reached in the absence of flocking behavior.

Follow the "Smart Money"

To be a successful trader, you must recognize the fact that you are competing against all other participants in the market. Accordingly, it is a good idea to monitor what other traders are up to and, more importantly, attempt to proactively guess what their next move might be.

As mentioned, large speculators (those with position sizes above the CFTC's reportable limits) are often referred to as the "smart money" simply because they are well capitalized and, in theory, they must have known what they were doing to get into the position they are in.

If the COT reveals that large speculators, also known as "reportables," have gone from long to short, it signals the category as a whole has grown bearish. This might be a good time for traders to *consider* following suit by looking for opportunities to play the currency from the short side. That said, it is never a good idea to blindly follow large speculators; they are only human, making errors in judgment possible, and likely have much deeper pockets than most small speculators. Simply put, those trading enough positions to fall into the reportable category typically have the luxury of less-than-perfect timing due to mass amounts of capital backing their speculation. If you can't ride out adversity like the large specs, following their lead could mean running the risk of being forced out of the trade before it ever becomes successful, if it ever does.

Fade the Small Specs?

Unfortunately, most futures and FX traders lose money; this is despite the fact that trading is nearly a zero-sum game. Ignoring the implication of transaction costs, for every winner there is a loser; mathematically, everyone should break even, but we all know that isn't true. Roughly 20% of market participants are making gains in the amount of the losses of the other 80%. Obviously, these are simplistic and rounded figures, but you get the idea.

> Take risks. If you win, you will be happy. If you lose, you will be wise.

For this reason, many analysts, including myself, look at the COT's "small speculator" category as a contrarian indicator. For instance, if small speculators are largely net long a market, it might be a good time to be a bear. Not only do they have a history of inaccurate speculation, but they also are fickle. This means they are likely to be late getting into the market and quick to liquidate once the tide turns; in addition, small speculators have a tendency to move together. The fickleness of small speculators is partly because they are working with limited capital, which triggers a propensity to place relatively tight stop loss orders to defend their positions. However, it is also because they are human and often chase markets and performance with hopes that previous price action will be indicative of future results.

Example of COT in an Overheated Market

Early in 2011, the Euro currency managed a magnificent rally against the U.S. Dollar that eventually ended up in disaster. Large hedge funds, CTAs, and even individual speculators believed that "money printing" by the Federal Reserve would be the demise of the greenback; accordingly they persistently and aggressively shorted the Dollar and bought Euro. However, as any trader will tell you, all good things eventually come to an end, and when they do the implications can be devastating for the complacent.

In Figure 11-5, you can see that the Commercial group consistently added to short positions as the Euro rallied and later offset their shorts as the market declined. Obviously, selling low and then buying back high is the exact opposite of what speculators are attempting to do. Nonetheless, although the "commercials" appear to be doing all the wrong things in the futures market, they are most likely doing all the right things in the SPOT market (business operations). In theory, if they have efficiently hedged their price risk, their losses in futures positions will be completely, or more, offset by gains in the SPOT market.

Courtesy of Barchart.com.

Figure 11-5   Traders should avoid following the Commercials category of the COT because their motive is to hedge price risk, not to profit from it in the futures markets. In fact, they often lose money in the futures markets but are simultaneously making money in the SPOT market (which isn't depicted by the COT).

On the other hand, markets with historically large net long or short positions among the large and small speculator categories of the COT are often an indicator of market capitulation and a looming price reversal. Simply put, a crowded trade has a tendency to end with a price spike in the direction of the trend as latecomers *panic to get into* the market out of fear of missing profits, and those on the wrong side of the move *panic to cut their losses.* This phenomenon is often called a **market squeeze** because it inflicts so much mental anguish and financial pain as poorly timed countertrend speculators are squeezed out of their positions.

> "The four most dangerous words in investing are 'This time it's different.'"
> —Sir John Templeton

Figure 11-6 depicts two instances in which the Euro currency experienced dramatic trend reversals following excessive net long and short positions held by the Large Speculator category of the COT. In May of 2011, large speculators were holding approximately 100,000 more long positions than short, and based on historical standards this is what could be considered an extremely lopsided position. After all, there is a buyer for every seller, and vice versa, so if the so-called smart money was holding more long contracts (to the tune of six digits) than short, there was a clear indication of overcrowding. Similarly, Figure 11-6 depicts a bottom found in the Euro in June of 2010 in which COT data revealed that large speculators were holding approximately 100,000 more short contracts than long.

Historically, large net long positions held by this group have meant at some point liquidation would occur to force prices lower as the bulls sold their contracts to square up obligations with the exchange. In essence, once all the bulls were in, there was only one way for them to get out: to sell. And that is exactly what they did! Once the wave of liquidation began, the June Euro futures contract fell precipitously from 1.4925 to 1.3963 in about two and a half weeks. This move equates to a profit or loss to a futures trader in the amount of $12,025 per standard-sized futures contract! Keep in mind, this phenomenon can happen just as easily in the reverse scenario; when Large Speculators amass signficant net short positions, they eventually have to buy their contracts back to offset their holdings. In such a case, the market is suceptible to a sharp short-covering rally.

> "If you want to have a better performance than the crowd, you must do things differently from the crowd."
> —Sir John Templeton

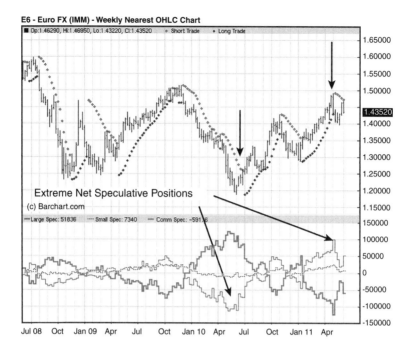

Figure 11-6 In early 2010, the Large Speculator group had amassed historically large net short positions, but a year later they had amassed the opposite, net long positions. This type of extreme market conviction often indicates a potential reversal.

You can see how easy it would be for complacent bulls to give back most of the profits from what was once a great trade—or, even worse, turn a winner into a loser in a matter of days. Simply being able to identify a crowded market could help you to avoid the inevitable pain and torture that lurks around the corner. If the idea of such supercharged profits and losses scares you, you can consider trading the mini Euro currency futures, which would have made or lost half of that of the standard, or $6,012.50. In Chapter 7, "Calculating in Currency Futures," we discuss E-micro futures, which are much smaller in regard to nominal size and therefore come with much less risk. The move described here translates into a profit or loss of $1,202.50 for an E-micro trader.

> "I can calculate the movement of the stars, but not the madness of men."
> —Sir Isaac Newton

Don't get wrapped up into thinking 100,000 is a magic number. The key to properly reading COT data is realizing that everything must be looked at on a relative basis. The number of open long or short contracts that constitutes an overheated market varies greatly from contract to contract, and from case to case. For instance, based on current market conditions at the time this book was going to print, 100,000 in the Euro seems to be a significantly extreme level but this might not always be true. In addition, markets with more or less open interest (traders with open positions) will see similar market moves on much different absolute net long and short numbers. For example, a sharp rally in the Japanese Yen was triggered by short covering and stop running following an overcrowded short trade in April of 2011; at the time the net short position was a mere 43,000. In comparison to the Euro, this seems moderate and hardly worth consideration, but relative to historical standards in the Yen, it was clear this was an overcrowded trade ripe for a turnaround.

Because COT stats are only useful when compared to historical values, the ability to see the net long or short positions visually depicted, as opposed to text data, can be imperative for COT readers to convert the information into proper trade and risk management.

Frankly, traders who find themselves victims of the wrath of a crowded trade gone bad are simply victims of their own greed, and I believe that monitoring the COT figures can help keep traders grounded by reality. The concept of a crowded trade is similar to that of a bubble in which the irrationality of the move can continue to excessive extremes but will undoubtedly end horribly. In fact, a bubble is just an extreme example of an overcrowded trade. Recognizing and avoiding trades the masses have dived into headfirst can do wonders toward preventing traders from being lured into the hype. Accordingly, they might avoid entering markets at inopportune times, or complacently allowing winning trades to quickly disintegrate. Of course, the opportunity cost of not following the crowd into overheated trades is not being able to participate in the water cooler stories at work regarding abnormal profits made in irrational runaway markets. Nonetheless, the bragging will almost always be silenced by the reality of the market…eventually.

How Can We Take Advantage of Seasonal Tendencies?

It is easy to understand that agricultural commodities such as grains could have distinct seasonal price patterns because their prices are based on variations in supply, demand, and harvest cycles. However, some are surprised to discover that similar seasonal tendencies occur in the financial markets and even currencies. The causes of the annual tendencies of these markets aren't as clear as those in raw commodities, but they do exist and could be helpful in steering traders clear of disastrous timing. Candidly, as a trader, that is all you need to know. Remember, traders should be looking to profit from the markets, not write a thesis.

Unfortunately, beginning traders often assume that making money is as easy as trading with the seasonal pattern and hoping for the best. However, it just isn't that easy. Before getting too excited, you should know that seasonal tendencies shouldn't be given much more credence than any other technical or fundamental analytical theory you might use in an attempt to predict market price. It is simply another tool in the trading tool belt; when combined with others, it might help you make decisions that are more educated.

> "Watch CNBC for entertainment, watch charts for trading."
> —Steve Burns

After all, even if seasonally bullish times of the year turn out to comply with the norm, there can be highly volatile counterseasonal moves that force traders out before they can enjoy the fruits of their labor. Additionally, it is important to realize that the markets (in the end) are efficient and its participants are all knowing. After all, we aren't the only people on the planet who can research seasonal tendencies. Accordingly, sometimes the moves occur early due to speculators anticipating certain price action, and at other times the move occurs late, after many have given up. The bottom line is, this information is useful, but it isn't the Holy Grail.

Ideally, as displayed in Figure 11-7, traders might feel more comfortable, and perhaps more aggressive, if their trade conforms to seasonality. On the other hand, traders shouldn't always avoid attempting counter seasonal trades if all other analysis lines up. Nevertheless, they shouldn't make a habit of it, and even more importantly, they should approach counter seasonal trades with a bit more conservatism than is normally the case.

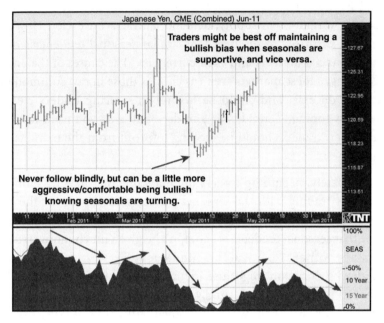

Charts provided by Gecko Software's Track N' Trade 5.0.

Figure 11-7 Seasonal tendencies aren't the Holy Grail of trading, but they can help traders determine an overall bias and aggression level.

Seasonal Trading Newsletters

A variety of seasonal newsletters are sold by analysts and distributed to traders. A majority of such services provide very specific trading recommendations, rather than simply displaying seasonal tendencies.

I cannot possibly speak specifically in regard to all seasonal newsletters and services, but similar to all other aspects in trading, there are never any guarantees of profit. Regardless of the source or how nice the paper the newsletter is printed on, all trading recommendations should be researched and confirmed accordingly. This does not mean you have to crunch historical numbers to confirm whether or not a market is bullish or bearish during a certain part of the year, but you should be aware of what has taken place in the previous few years and consider other forms of analysis to confirm your stance.

Many seasonal services will provide entry and exit dates, along with the rate of success over a certain time period, usually 15 years. They may also give you the average gain or loss for the trade over the same span of time. However, what you may not be able to see is the drawdown that the trade suffered between the entry and exit date. Simply put, the entry and exit date provide a snapshot of the recommended position and how it has averaged based on those exact two instances in the past. On the other hand, what happens in between these points is unknown and could be very significant. In fact, some small traders might have run out of money before the trade completed itself...possibly at a profit.

I'm not suggesting that you completely avoid seasonal trading newsletters that provide trading recommendations in the aforementioned format, but you should certainly approach the strategy with caution. After all, if making money in the currency markets was as easy as identifying seasonal patterns and buying or selling on certain days of the year, they wouldn't be selling the information to you or me. Bluntly, there is much more money to be made in the vast currency markets than there is in the sales of newsletters or trading software.

Simple risk management strategies such as placing stops or, better yet, using protective option spread plays may be a wiser approach. Also, additional fundamental and technical analysis should be conducted to verify your agreement with the recommendation.

> The market is out to get everyone. Success lies in knowing and respecting this.

As an avid follower of the futures and FX markets, I believe very strongly in having access to historical market data and a source of seasonal tendencies. A simple and affordable source of seasonal guidance is the *Commodity Trader's Almanac.* I would never recommend initiating a trade based on seasonality alone, but as a rule of thumb, I wouldn't necessarily recommend trading against it either...unless of course there is a great opportunity.

12

Getting Technical with Currencies

S imilar to technical analysts in any other market, currency technicians attempt to predict price changes via the study of historical price and volume data. The concept of such analysis contradicts what is typically taught in college finance courses and the assumption that market prices are completely random. However, technical analysis can be a valuable tool to predict the timing of short-term market moves. In fact, I believe traders are best off using fundamental analysis (including seasonals and COT) to determine a bias, but entry and exit should be guided by technical factors. After all, markets are all-knowing and therefore "waiting" to hear or confirm the news for yourself will likely mean you are too late.

I could feasibly write a small series of books on technical analysis and still be forced to leave critical information out for the sake of print space. However, it is worthwhile to scratch the surface of the topic simply because it is important to be aware of the basic chart patterns that other traders (that is, your competition) might be focused on. Also, in light of the short-term nature of most currency-trading literature, online services, and other educational outlets, you need to be familiar with some of the basic technical tools and terminology. Should you opt to use technical analysis in your trading, you can take the base knowledge learned in this chapter and focus on application and details through more focused texts and paper trading accounts.

Unfortunately, there isn't a single chart formation, technical oscillator, or charting tool that will lead traders to automatic success. Technical analysis in currency trading is a highly skilled art that must be cultivated and will likely involve the use of a refined tool belt rather than a single tool.

Throughout my years in close proximity to the markets, I've concluded that each trading decision should be based on a combination of technical confirmations, in corroboration with fundamental and seasonal factors. More specifically, I believe traders should form market opinions based on all three analytical studies (seasonal, fundamental, technical), but timing market entry and exit is probably best done via chart work. After all, simply being right about market direction doesn't guarantee profits; timing is everything!

Not All Currency Technicians Are Created Equal

Within the realm of technical analysis are several schools of thought with vastly different methodologies. Among the most commonly referred to are trend trading, breakout trading, and countertrend trading. This isn't an exhaustive list, but should give you an idea of how others might be strategizing.

Trend Traders

In its simplest form, trend trading often involves using relatively slow entry and exit triggers based on technical oscillators and moving averages. Because of the nature of the analysis and strategy, trend traders are typically slow to buy into a rally and therefore often buy the highs of a move. Conversely, they are often late sellers into a bear market and have a tendency to sell an already low price in hopes of the market going *even lower*. Unfortunately for trend traders, due to lagging entry signals, they face dismal odds of success on a per-trade basis, but the premise of the strategy lies in the expectations of eventually catching a dramatic market move in which the gains are so significant they offset the frequent losses that took place before catching a ride in the market.

> The premise of trend trading is to buy high and sell higher, and to sell low and sell lower.

Breakout Traders

Breakout traders tend to focus on trendiness combined with trading channels, and attempt to profit from a currency that breaks above resistance or below support. Such traders are assuming a break of technical barriers will lead to a continuation of the move. Breakout traders are similar to trend traders in that they require the market to move in the intended direction before they are willing to enter. Accordingly, this strategy comes with the same difficulties faced by trend traders; buying at high prices and selling at low prices. Nonetheless, should the market actually continue to move following the technical breach of support or resistance, the gains could be significant. Like trend trading, this approach to trading offers traders relatively low odds of success for each given trade, but the hope is to catch a big enough winner to return a profit despite numerous losses beforehand.

> "I believe the very best money is made at the market turns. Everyone says you get killed trying to pick tops and bottoms and you make all your money by playing the trend in the middle. Well, for twelve years I have been missing the meat in the middle but I have made a lot of money at tops and bottoms."
> —Paul Tudor Jones

Countertrend Traders

Although it goes against human nature, and isn't necessarily the most popular approach, I believe the most efficient means of technical analysis might be in relation to countertrend trading. In other words, rather than using tools and indicators to identify a trend and go with it, traders might be better off determining overextended market conditions and trading against the tide. If the goal is to buy low and sell high (which it should be), being bullish near technical support and bearish near resistance should offer the best odds of success. This theory could be even more valid in markets such as the currencies, which typically trade within long-term

> Support and resistance represent the price at which supply and demand meet. Specifically, **support** is the level traders feel demand (buyers) will increase enough to prevent further declines. **Resistance** is the area traders believe supply (sellers) will increase to prevent further price gains.

ranges, as opposed to perpetual bull and bear markets, although there can certainly be relentless intermediate-term trends.

Renowned trader Peter Lynch once had the following to say about trading in the stock market: "The one principle that applies to nearly all these so-called 'technical approaches' is that one should buy because a stock, or the market, has gone up, and one should sell because it has declined. This is the exact opposite of sound business sense everywhere else, and it is most unlikely that it can lead to lasting success in Wall Street. In our own stock-market experience and observation, extending over 50 years, we have not known a single person who has consistently, or lastingly, made money by thus 'following the market.' We do not hesitate to declare that this approach is as fallacious as it is popular."

Technical Technology

With technological advances in trading has come increased access to market information and technical tools for the average retail trader. Paper charts with penciled trend lines are a thing of the past—although Jim Cramer, a popular trading television host, claims to still use them. Traders now have electronic charting and the luxury of instant and effortless mathematical indicators to measure trend and momentum. Similarly, thanks to computers, trend lines can be drawn, and redrawn, repeatedly as prices change.

Although more information and convenient analysis seems like it could be an advantage, I'm not convinced that it is. With the exception of proprietary indicators (developed in-house or by an individual trader and not made available to the public), nearly every trader has access to the same computer-generated oscillators and technical trading tools. Therefore, it is unlikely that simply following an indicator would produce positive trading results in the long haul. If trading were that easy there would be no need for any of us to work for a living, because that would mean there would be virtually no risk in trading.

I strongly believe the difference between success and failure isn't determined by which indicators you choose to use (or not to use) but how you use them. In other words, similar to most activities in life, I estimate trading success to be 90% attributed to mental stability and only 10% market analysis. Nonetheless, technical analysis plays a large part in the decision-making process for most traders and shouldn't be taken for granted.

Computer-Generated Oscillators and Indicators

The most commonly used tool in technical analysis is the computer-generated oscillator, simply referred to as an **indicator.** Its popularity stems from its simplicity; there is little work involved in the application of indicators, and interpretation is relatively straightforward.

> "Where you want to be is always in control, never wishing, always trading, and always, first and foremost, protecting your butt."
> —Paul Tudor Jones

As the name implies, an indicator's purpose is to attempt to "indicate" the direction of the market. As charting moved from paper to the computer screen, the number of technical oscillators exploded. A nearly unlimited number of technical indicators are available; many advanced charting software packages enable traders to create their own indicators based on self-stipulated parameters. Nonetheless, all indicators have at least two things in common:

- Contrary to the name, indicators tell traders what the market has already done and not necessarily what it will do in the future.

- Although tempting, technical indicators should not be followed blindly.

Perhaps my opinion on the usefulness of indicators is a bit controversial. I argue that despite the variable parameters of each technical indicator, in the long run traders would have approximately the same success blindly executing signals derived from one particular indicator as they would any of the others. In other words, I don't think any single indicator is more accurate than another; they simply perform differently in various time frames, market conditions, and strategies. Depending on the inputs and the mathematical equations driving computer-generated oscillators, some will react to market movement quicker than others. This causes a higher quantity of trading signals with significant levels of aggression. Swing traders, or those looking to profit from relatively brief ebbs and flow of price movement, often use these quicker indicators.

Some of the popular computer-generated oscillators worth noting are Williams Percent R, RSI, Stochastics, and the MACD. When used in conjunction with each other, these oscillators can be valuable. Naturally, this isn't meant to be an exhaustive list, and an oscillator being excluded from it doesn't necessarily deem the oscillator worthless. The key is to find which of them work best with your trading strategy, risk tolerance, and personality. I've personally witnessed multiple traders using the same technical indicators to determine when to enter and exit a market who yield dramatically different results. The discrepancy is likely due to the manner in which the traders were able to manage their emotions. Therefore, picking a basket of indicators you trust and are comfortable with will work toward reducing unnecessary emotional turmoil in yourself.

Williams Percent R (%R)

If you've read any trading books at all, you're expected to have run across the infamous Larry Williams. Williams won the 1987 World Cup Championship of Futures Trading, where he turned $10,000, in real money, into over $1,100,000 (11,376%) in a 12-month competition. Mr. Williams created the Williams %R indicator with the same intentions of most technical indicators—to identify oversold and overbought market conditions.

The Williams %R involves calculations that consider the current market price, compared to where the commodity has been in the previous 10 sessions. The indicator is depicted as a single line drawn between the values of 20% and 80%. Once the line crosses above or below the noted percentages, the market is deemed to be overheated or undervalued. Depending on the strategy employed, this might mean a signal to traders who have caught the move to exit with a profit, or countertrend traders might see it as a signal to enter the market in the opposite direction of the trend. In my opinion, traders are best off patiently waiting for prices to be discounted before buying and overvalued before selling. This indicator is one of the helpful tools that can be used to determine such conditions. As tempting as it might be, buying a futures

> The financial markets are the only place where people aren't comfortable buying things on "sale," but in many cases that is exactly when they should be!

when the %R is above 80% could prove to be disaster should a correction ensue. Pullbacks in an overbought market can be fierce. On the other hand, you might be asking yourself, if every time the market is oversold it should be bought and every time it is overbought it should be sold, how does it make any progress? The truth is, this is a valid concern, and it is a good reminder that overbought and oversold indicators don't offer any guarantees when it comes to accuracy.

It has been said that markets spend about 80% of the time trading within a range and 20% of the time re-pricing. Clearly, indicators such as the Williams %R will be less useful during the 20% of the time in which prices are on the move. In such circumstances, a market can remain overbought or oversold (as determined by common indicators) for quite some time. Should this occur, countertrend traders will suffer losses whereas trend traders, and possibly breakout traders, will likely be enjoying the fruits of their patient labor.

I'm not insinuating that overbought and oversold indicators are accurate exactly 80% of the time, but I'd guess that it is somewhere between 60% and 80%. Therefore, if you think profitable trading is as simple as following a basic computer-generated oscillator, you might want to go back to the drawing board.

Please note that the most common version of Williams %R is stated in inverse values. For simplicity, I like to use the version of the indicator that suggests a market is overbought if its %R line is above 80% and oversold if it is below 20%. However, Figure 12-1 displays the version in which a reading above 20% suggests the rally could be exhausted and a reading below 80% signifies oversold pricing.

RSI (Relative Strength Index)

Similar to Williams %R, RSI is most often used to determine overbought and oversold conditions and can be applied to a particular currency pair or currency futures contract. This indicator was developed by J. Welles Wilder, Jr. and is depicted as a single line with monetary values ranging between 100 and 0. In general, an RSI value in excess of 70% suggests an overheated rally and a value below 30% signals oversold market conditions (see Figure 12-2).

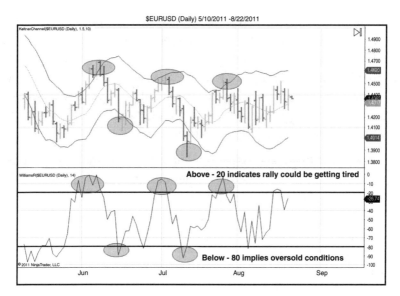

Charts created with BESTDirect NinjaTrader Software.

Figure 12-1 %R values below 20% signal overbought conditions and could be followed by selling pressure (profit taking). Values above 80% suggest the market is oversold and a short covering rally is possible.

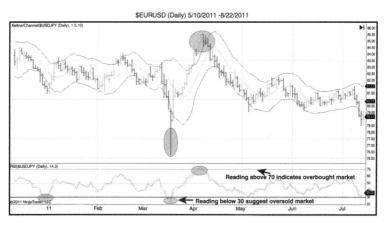

Charts created with BESTDirect NinjaTrader Software.

Figure 12-2 Slower than the %R, the RSI might offer traders more reliable signals. Above 70% suggests the market is overbought, and below 30% oversold.

For many, a crossover from below 30% to above 30% is considered a buy signal and a crossover from above 70% to below is viewed as a sell signal.

However, depending on the strategy and level of aggression, traders might consider any value beyond these points as an opportune time to enter the market in the opposite direction of the trend, rather than waiting for a crossover of the indicator back above 30% or below 70%.

Before indicators such as Williams %R and RSI can be useful to traders, they must first understand how these indicators perform relative to each other. For instance, RSI is a much slower indicator than the Williams %R; this means that it will deem a market to be oversold or overbought much later than %R. Because of this, it is possible that this indicator will miss some trading opportunities purely because it is too slow to identify a possible reversal. However, it will also produce fewer false signals than a quicker indicator, such as %R, might.

Because it is a slower indicator, I believe the RSI to be an optimal choice for timing trade entry. After all, successful trading requires putting the odds in your favor, and patience is usually a virtue. In other words, waiting for the RSI to produce a signal could mean a higher probability trade; this is because traders will be buying "cheaper" due to the delay in producing a signal relative to the Williams %R . For instance, traders might use a quicker indicator such as Stochastics (discussed next) or %R as a "get ready" and confirmation of the RSI as a "go."

Slow Stochastics

Despite its title, Slow Stochastics (typically referred to Stochastics) is a moderately quick-paced oscillator. Slow Stochastics is dubbed as "slow" because relative to its cousin, Fast Stochastics (sometimes referred to as Regular Stochastics), it is. I'm not a big advocate of using Fast Stochastics merely because I believe the pace of the indicator leads to a high frequency of false signals. For the opposite reasoning, I believe the Slow Stochastics is a more reliable technical tool because it is essentially a smoothed version of the Fast Stochastics calculation. The smoothing factor leads to less noise, less confusion, and less trigger-happy trading.

Developed by Dr. George C. Lane, the Slow Stochastic measures the closing price of a currency futures or FX pair relative to its price range over a given period. This measure is represented in a percentage format, but unlike the RSI and Williams %R, Stochastics is depicted by *two lines*. These lines are known as %K and %D. The former is the measure of

---

market momentum based on closing price and the high and low of the previous 14 price bars. The latter is a three-bar moving average of the %K. A crossover of the lines is considered a buy or sell signal, with the most reliable being those that occur above 80% or below 20% (see Figure 12-3).

As the saying goes, "Markets can stay irrational longer than most can stay solvent."

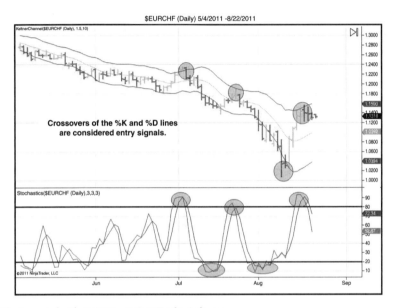

Charts created with BESTDirect NinjaTrader Software.

Figure 12-3   Any crossover of the %K and %D lines is interpreted as a signal, but signals occuring above the 80% line or below the 20% line are considered more reliable.

If the market has rallied too far too fast and the closing price is near the upper end of its scale, the indicator will have a value approaching 100%. In a market that has fallen sharply and is experiencing closing prices near the bottom of the range, the value of the Slow Stochastics will be near 0%. The original calculation is based on 14 periods (price bars), but the parameters can be adjusted to speed up or slow down the indicator.

The market is said to be "embedded" if it remains overbought (above 80%) or oversold (below 20%) for several trading sessions. Once a market is embedded, as deemed by Slow Stochastics, it can remain that way for a substantial amount of time, and therefore negates the likelihood of an accurate signal.

MACD (Moving Average Convergence Divergence)

Created by Gerald Appel to measure the strength of a long-term trend, the MACD considers the difference between two exponential moving averages with various time periods as inputs.

Because the averages used in the computation are weighted, also known as "exponential," the output tends to be smoother than indicators whose value is based on simple moving averages.

> Trading success isn't determined by how much money you make, but how much you don't lose.

Specifically, the MACD is the computed difference between the two moving averages and is most often depicted as a histogram with a zero value as the baseline. However, you might see it displayed as lines, or even a combination of the two (see Figure 12-4).

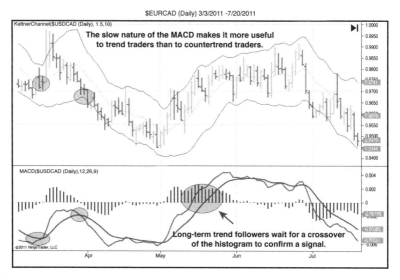

Charts created with BESTDirect NinjaTrader Software.

Figure 12-4 The MACD is one of the slower-paced indicators available to traders. Aggressive traders see any line crossover as an entry signal, but trend traders opt to wait for a crossover of the lines through the zero mark.

Conservative traders, or those seeking additional confirmation before entering a trade, consider a crossover of the histogram through the zero line as a trading signal. However, traders who are more active look at a crossover of the moving average lines in the direction of the histogram, or on the histogram's crossover zero, as an entry signal.

The MACD is a comparatively slow-paced oscillator. In my estimation, it is best used to confirm a trend and to identify the maturity of the trend. Perhaps other oscillators might be better suited to determine the timing of trade entry.

Popular Advanced Charting Tools

Computer-generated oscillators are popular because they require little input from the user. In fact, using indicators is as simple as instructing charting software to calculate the values and provide you with the results visually—usually in vibrant colors and an easy-to-read format. Advanced charting tools, on the other hand, are based on theory more than they are mathematics, and are open to dramatic differences in interpretation. Nonetheless, they are similar to computer-generated oscillators in that they are only as good as the trader using them.

Fibonacci Ruler

Although those in the trading community have been familiar with Fibonacci and his mathematical theories for some time, many were introduced to the topic in the recent decade. Books, movies, and video games such as *The Da Vinci Code* brought Fibonacci to the mainstream. For those who haven't seen the movie or read the book, Leonardo Fibonacci (aka Leonardo Pisano and Leonardo Bonacci) was an Italian mathematician.

Considered by many to be among the most talented figures of the Middle Ages, Fibonacci was responsible for introducing the **Fibonacci sequence.** In the sequence of numbers, each number is the sum of its previous two numbers, starting with 0 and 1. Here's the beginning of the sequence:

0, 1, 1, 2, 3, 5, 8, 13, 21, 34, 55, 89, 144, 233, 377, 610, 987, and so on

As the sequence progresses, two consecutive numbers divided by each other will produce what is known as the "Golden Ratio," or 61.8%. For example, dividing 610 by 987 equals 0.618034448. According to Fibonacci theory, nature, and therefore market prices, tend to move in increments in line with this ratio (see Figure 12-5).

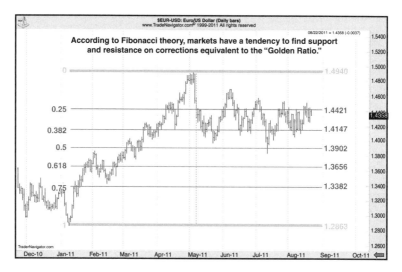

Charts created with BESTDirect Navigator by Genesis Software.

Figure 12-5 According to Fibonacci theory, markets tend to find support or resistance after retracing 50% to 61.8% of a market move.

Specifically, the theory suggests market moves will find support or resistance after retracing the following percentages of the initial move:

- 23.6% (found by dividing any number in the sequence by the number that is three places to the right)

- 38.2% (found by dividing any number in the sequence by the number that is found two places to the right)

- 50% (the midpoint between high and low)

- 61.8% (found by dividing any number in the sequence by the number that immediately follows it)

- 76.4% (found by subtracting 0.236 from the number 1)

Conventional use of the Fibonacci ruler in trading involves stretching it from a major market high to low, or vice versa. The ruler assumes a countertrend move is somewhat temporary, or will at least struggle to surpass certain points.

You will find variations of the Fibonacci ruler in regard to the number of applicable levels, but most traders use a ruler with all five of the areas of support or resistance noted in the above ratios. The last and first retracement areas, 23.6% and 76.4%, are considered to be less reliable than the others; it is the Golden Ratio of 61.8% that is given the most credence. Although expecting market prices to magically reverse at such an arbitrary level seems mystical and illogical, there does seem to be some "magic" to it. That said, there is also a bit of self-fulfilling prophecy in that if you draw enough lines on the chart, one of them is bound to appear as though it is acting as support and resistance. This is exactly why some traders, and some Fibonacci rulers, eliminate the less reliable first and fifth retracement levels.

Elliot Wave

Elliot Wave theory is popular among technicians, but like economists, each Elliot Wave theorist has a relatively unique prediction. As is the case with trading in general, use of such a tool is an art rather than a science; this leaves many shades of gray with little black and white.

Developed by Ralph Nelson Elliot, Elliot Wave theory states that market behavior is determined by waves of bullish and bearish sentiment, rather than random timing. In other words, those holding to the theory believe that human nature is somewhat predictable, and because prices are a reflection of trader psychology, identifiable patterns exist. Not only did Elliot believe market participants continually react to changes in the market in a predictable fashion, but he claimed that prices rose and fell based on the Golden Ratio.

Elliot Wave theory claims the market rises in a series of five alternating waves and declines in a series of three alternating waves. Specifically, the market rises on the first wave, declines on the second, rallies into wave three, but is followed by a declining wave four, and finally completes the rally on wave five. Of these waves, the third is often the most powerful, but wave five tends to be the largest and is the final leg in the direction of the dominant trend. Unfortunately, it is the fifth wave that often attracts traders who are simply late to the party, and they are often met with a painful three-wave correction, referred to as A, B, and C (see Figure 12-6).

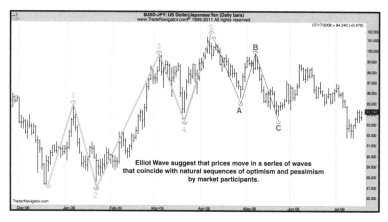

Charts created with BestDirect Navigator by Genesis Software.

Figure 12-6 Properly identifying waves can be difficult in real time and isn't necessarily beneficial after the fact.

There isn't a shortage of trading newsletters, traders, and analysts who claim to have made a living focusing on Elliot Wave. Nonetheless, there are downfalls, and the tool is open to vast amounts of subjective interpretation. For instance, traders using a Fibonacci retracement ruler to try to predict the size of a current wave could have difficulty doing so until after the fact. After all, even moves that comply with Fibonacci theory, as Elliot intended, can see retracements of either 23.6%, 38.2%, 50%, 61.8% or 76.4% and the difference between the first and the last can be massive in regard to a trader's profit and loss.

Accordingly, I believe it can be difficult to base entry and exit points using Elliot Wave theory. As is the case with any other trading tool, this theory should be applied in conjunction with other technical analysis instruments or indicators.

Gann Fan

For those of you who miss using protractors and the study of geometric angles, the Gann Fan will keep you busy for a while. This is one of those market theories that has reached cult status in the currency trading world; I am almost certain its popularity has more to do with intrigue than usefulness.

Originally created by W.D. Gann, the Gann Fan incorporates the use of geometric angles in conjunction with time and price. According to Gann, certain geometric patterns can be used to predict price movement.

Thanks to electronic charting capabilities, traders no longer have to draw Gann Fans with protractors and rulers. However, although charting software will allow traders to draw Gann Fans in a nearly unlimited number of ways, Gann intended for the fan to be drawn with equal time and price intervals. If done correctly, a rise in one unit of price by one unit of time is equal to a 45-degree angle. According to the theory, this one-to-one relationship is ideal for keeping proper balance between price and time. Naturally, markets don't always follow Gann's idea of balance, but the fan helps to determine areas of support and resistance, which might influence prices to retreat back to the 45-degree range. As the market passes through one fan line, prices should move to the next (see Figure 12-7). Each angle in the fan is labeled by its relationship of time over price—for example, 1×8 (1 time unit by 8 price units), 1×4, and so on.

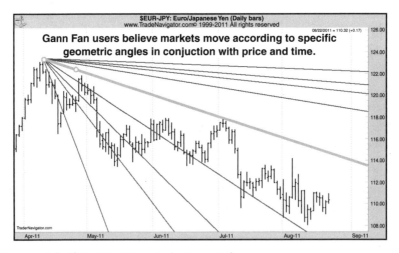

Charts created with BestDirect Navigator by Genesis Software.

Figure 12-7   Gann Fans use angles and geometry to attempt to identify possible levels of support and resistance.

According to Gann Fan theory, the fan should stem from a major market high or low and be drawn with the center fan line on a 45-degree angle. Like Elliot Wave, Gann Fan analysis leaves much of the instrument drawing and interpretation to the discretion of the trader. In my opinion, the Gann Fan is helpful in enabling traders to take a step back to look at the big picture and the various levels that could provide support and resistance. Nonetheless, trading solely from a Gann Fan is difficult to do.

Drawing Trend Lines and Channels

Many beginning traders overlook the benefits of understanding trend lines and channels simply because they aren't as exciting as high-tech mathematical oscillators or mythical theories such as the Gann Fan or Fibonacci retracements. Nonetheless, these simple tools can be among the most effective in analyzing a market.

Conceivably another turnoff for many is the fact that drawing trend lines on a chart is more of an art than a science. That is because there really isn't one way to do it, and chances are that each trader will have a slightly different idea of where and how one should be drawn. In addition, many trending markets have two trend lines, known as internal and external. For those who are mathematically inclined, and feel there should be a black-and-white answer for every problem, trend lines might seem arbitrary and too easy to be true. However, in my judgment, there is a significant benefit in using them.

The premise of drawing trend lines is to determine areas of support and resistance, which might encourage price reversals. Regardless of the strategy utilized, such information is critical to success. For instance, breakout traders might look at trend lines as the area that confirms the beginning of a "break out" from a trading channel, yet range traders might look at the support and resistance areas provided by trend lines as the place to buy the dip or sell the rally. You shouldn't be surprised by the vast difference in views of what trend lines might mean to prices; don't forget, for every winner there is a loser. If everyone looked at markets in the same manner, there wouldn't be a market at all.

Unfortunately, trend lines tend to be general areas of support and resistance rather than exact. Beginning traders often make the mistake of assuming a price print a few ticks beyond the drawn trend line is equivalent to a technical violation that can never be repaired. On the contrary, trend lines are often temporarily broken before proving to eventually be valid support or resistance. Simply put, although trend lines are a useful guide, traders shouldn't expect that market penetration of a trend line they drew on their chart will guarantee a large price movement. Sometimes, markets test trend lines and even temporarily puncture them before resuming the trend; this simply means the trend line needs to be redrawn. As you can see, trend lines are another tool to aid in the decision-making process, but like all the tools available, they should be used in combination with other indicators and technical analysis apparatus.

Trend lines are like opinions—everyone has one and few agree with each other. Nonetheless, in its simplest form, a trend line in an inclining market should be drawn along the lowest points of the price bars. Trend lines in declining markets are drawn through the high price points of the trend.

The more instances in which prices bounce off the trend line, the more relevant it becomes as a prediction tool. Similarly, all trend lines must start somewhere. It takes as few as two points to draw a trend line, but I wouldn't recommend putting too much faith into a trend at such an early stage. In fact, popular theory suggests that at least three points touching a trend line are necessary to "confirm" its validity. Also, a steep trend in either direction shouldn't be viewed as reliable; after all, according to Gann Fan theory, markets move in 45-degree angles. Whether or not the exact geometry applies, it's relatively rare for a market in free fall or a parabolic rally to continue to trade in such a manner for extended lengths of time. Steep trends are often temporary and followed by dramatic reversals; you don't want to be in the wrong place at the wrong time! What goes up will eventually go down faster; there is a famous quip in the financial world that states the market rallies up stairs but goes down in an elevator.

A trend channel consists of a section of price bars in which definitive lines can be drawn through the highs of the range as well as the lows. In other words, the market is obeying a definitive trend line on the inclines as well as the declines. Naturally, a trend channel can be sideways (parallel support and resistance), inclining (upward-slanting support and resistance), or declining (downward-sloping support and resistance). Trend channels might also be narrowing or widening as market volatility fluctuates from high to low, or vice versa.

Regardless of the shape of the channel, the premise of the technical theory assumes the bottom line represents support and the top line acts as resistance. Swing traders use such channels as entry points for price speculation against the upper or lower line of the channel, but breakout traders look for penetration of either the price ceiling or floor in anticipation of a much bigger move (see Figure 12-8).

Charts created with BestDirect Navigator by Genesis Software.

Figure 12-8 Swing traders determine entry prices near support and resistance based on trend channels; breakout traders look for penetration of the channel for entry signals.

Currencies Gap!

Some beginning traders come to the currency markets to avoid the horrors of price gaps they've heard commodity traders struggle with, but the truth is, gaps can't be completely escaped. That said, although this type of price action does occur in the futures and FOREX markets today, it is much less common than it used to be.

A **price gap** occurs when there is a significant difference in the closing price of the previous trading session relative to the opening price of the next session. Gaps can be either up or down, and are simply coined as a "gap up" or a "gap down." You might even hear "gap higher" or "gap lower."

Because currency futures contracts trade *virtually* 24 hours per day, and the FOREX markets are in operation exactly 24 hours per day during the week, there simply isn't much of an opportunity for many large price gaps. Naturally, there are exceptions; at times, there is some event or newly discovered information that changes the market's perception of currency value during the downtime. Remember, currency futures trading through the CME Group are closed from 4:00 p.m. Central to 5:00 p.m. Central, Monday through Thursday. Although it is not common, it is entirely possible that currency prices will change dramatically during this hour and the result will be a price gap at the reopen of trade. Figure 12-9 depicts an extreme example of such a gap that occurred in the Japanese Yen in the spring of 2011.

Charts provided by Gecko Software's Track N' Trade 5.0.

Figure 12-9 Hours before the IMM intervened in the currency markets in March of 2011, the Yen was rallying uncontrollably as funds flowed into the currency in the form of aid to help repair Japan after a devastating earthquake.

The absence of mid-week gaps, albeit rare in futures, is an advantage to trading currencies in the FOREX market. With that in mind, traders holding positions over the weekend in either arena will be subject to risk of substantial gaps. This makes sense because currency trading of all types ceases on Friday evening and doesn't resume until Sunday evening. For instance, the Euro seems to gap higher or lower 10 to 20 pips rather frequently, but I have seen instances when the gap is 80 or more pips. To clarify the meaning of a gap, if the EUR/USD closes at 1.4150 on the Friday close and opens up Sunday evening at 1.4185, the market is said to have gapped higher by 35 pips.

As we all know, a lot can happen in a few days, and Friday's assumed reality might have completely altered by the resumption of the next week's trading. During the two-day hiatus, it is possible that domestic or international political events have developed, a natural disaster has occurred, or some other event has taken place that will potentially influence pricing. Accordingly, gaps higher or lower from the Friday close are somewhat frequent.

Trading Price Gaps

There's no shortage of articles, books, and even courses dedicated solely to gap trading. Although I cannot get into detail here, I believe it is important for traders to be familiar with what others might be thinking. The theory is that most gaps, perhaps 80% or more, are filled. Being filled simply means that once the price gap is established, the market trades back through the gap to retest support or resistance identified as the price where the gap started (the previous close). Because currencies tend to be range-bound markets rather than bull or bear, in the long run I'd have to agree that most gaps are filled. Of course, like anything in speculative trading, timing is everything. The market sometimes fills a gap within a single trading session (see Figure 12-10), or in a few days, but other times it takes weeks or months.

Knowing this, some traders try to "fade the gap" by trading in the opposite direction of it. For instance, if the market gaps higher, some traders might look to be sellers in anticipation of the gap being filled via a price decline to the place the gap started. On a gap lower, some traders will be looking to buy into the move, expecting the price to increase back to the point where the gap began. Conversely, some gap traders look to enter the market in the direction of the gap, but after the gap has already been filled. Specifically, a market that gaps higher might offer traders with an opportunity to buy once the price retests support, marked by the previous close prior to the gap.

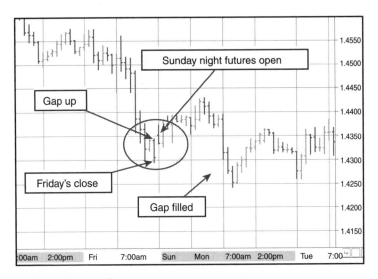

Courtesy of QST charting software.

Figure 12-10   Gap traders sometimes view a price gap higher on the open of trade as an opportunity to sell the currency in hopes of the gap getting filled. After the gap is filled, some traders consider this a signal to enter the market in the direction of the gap.

One thing is certain: For a gap to occur, there has to be an overwhelming shift in market bias and more often than not you probably don't want to fight the move too aggressively. Once again, you will always find dissenting views in the financial markets, but that is what makes a market a market.

Keep It Simple, Stupid (KISS)

Although this chapter merely introduces the topic of technical analysis, it's important to be aware of the basic premise of the concept. Not only might it help you to understand price movement, but it will give you an idea of what your competition might be thinking. Additionally, a basic knowledge of various technical tools available to traders might help you discover the avenue you would like to explore in more detail.

It is never a good idea to rely on only one or two technical tools, but it is equally challenging to interpret the meaning of several at a time. The sheer mass of available computer-generated oscillators and mathematical theories floating around the trading world is often overwhelming. Unfortunately, the result is often "analysis paralysis" and therefore a lot of "shoulda, coulda, woulda" frustration.

I believe traders are prone to overcomplicating technical analysis, and this, in turn, works against the goal of successful trading. Markets are dynamic and, therefore, analysis of them should be looked at as an art and not a science. What works today might not work tomorrow; as a result, traders might be better off focusing on the mental aspects of market speculation as opposed to the technical. After all, as a trader, you will be competing against all other market participants. Each and every one of you is sharing the same access to the same fundamental information and technical tools, but the one thing you have that others don't is what is between your ears!

13

Tips and Tricks for Currency Traders

T here are nearly as many trading strategies as there are traders, but in the world of currencies, it seems as though the most common form of speculation is day trading. The term **day trading** simply implies that traders enter positions with the intention of being flat with the market by the close. In other words, it is the practice of entering and exiting speculative positions within a single trading day.

"Money grows on the tree of persistence."
—Japanese proverb

Even within the realm of day trading lies a nearly unlimited number of methodologies. For instance, some day traders attempt to scalp a few ticks on each trade by rapidly entering and exiting trades in the blink of an eye; yet others hold positions for several hours hoping to profit from larger price moves. Regardless of the time horizon and profit target, the goal is the same: to make money. Unfortunately, the odds are stacked sorely against currency day traders, but those who manage to gain the skills and experience necessary to be successful stand to be handsomely rewarded. On balance, ignoring transaction costs, for every losing trade in FX there is a winning trade, and stats suggest there are far more losers than winners. If most people are losing money, those who are on the opposite end of the spectrum must be doing very well.

Despite the challenges, traders are often drawn to day trading because it provides them with low barriers to entry, it lacks the overnight risk position traders endure, and, let's face it, day trading is exciting. The idea of speeding up your trading results is appealing; after all, you will likely use the same technical indicators and oscillators for day trading as you would position trading, so why wait weeks for the outcome? Instead, you can determine whether you have what it takes to make money within a single trading day.

> "The only place you find success before work is in the dictionary."
> —Unknown entrepreneur

Being within the trading industry for several years has provided me the privilege of having a front row seat to the game of retail trading. Based on my observations, day trading is prone to be one of the most difficult strategies to employ successfully. Yet, with difficulty comes potential reward for those who are capable of managing emotions and willing to put the time in to pay their "experience" dues to the market.

Once again, I believe it is fair to say that trading is more of an art than a science. In other words, there isn't a single formula for success. I have been a commodity broker since early 2004 and I have yet to see a strategy or system that works in all market conditions. The truth is, markets are dynamic and what works in one environment might not work in another. Additionally, what works for one trader might not work for the next; I've witnessed traders armed with the same trade recommendation (entry and exit pricing included) experience vastly different results. From scenarios such as this, I estimate that the difference between success and failure isn't the oscillator you choose to use, or even the trading strategy; instead, it is the ability to stay calm during adverse market movements and logical during favorable. Unfortunately, this is much easier said than done.

This chapter discusses a few of the most common mental mistakes made by day traders.

It Takes Money to Make Money

Whether you opt to trade currencies in the futures or FX markets, one thing is constant: There is plenty of leverage available to anybody who is willing to take the plunge. At the risk of being repetitive, currency futures traders are granted ultra-low day-trading margin rates, whereas FX clients (those in the U.S. anyway) are limited to the NFA's cap of a 50-to-1 leverage ratio. Nonetheless, in either venue, traders are free to take large speculative positions with relatively little money on deposit.

Unfortunately, many FX and futures brokerage firms focus marketing efforts on luring traders to the markets with the benefits of leverage. The truth is, too much leverage doesn't give traders an advantage, it gives them an incredible burden, and dismally low probabilities of success. This is because over-leveraged traders are often forced out of positions prematurely in the midst of normal ebb-and-flow price changes due to a lack of margin or funds. On the other hand, a trader who doesn't utilize all the leverage granted to her might have the financial and mental wherewithal to withstand the adverse price movement that precedes favorable movement. Simply put, *less leverage* directly translates into *more room for error,* and I think it is fair to say that this alone betters the odds of success. After all, I'm not perfect, and chances are, neither are you. The "less perfect" we have to be to walk away a winner, the better off we are.

Keep in mind, in the case of futures accounts, many of the discount firms offering low margins are quick to liquidate client positions should their account equity dip (even slightly) below the stated day-trading margin rate. Further, in such a circumstance, not only is the room for error limited to the capital in your trading account, but it might be limited to the amount of intraday margin your brokerage firm requires you to have on deposit. Violations of the broker's set intraday margin rates might result in the forced liquidation of positions. I can tell you first hand, you never want to leave the results of your trading up to your broker's risk management department or to computerized auto-liquidation as some FX firms use. Also, paying a few extra dollars in commission to trade with a futures broker that is a little more lenient with day-trading margin might save you a lot of money in the long run.

Once a trader allows his positions to get to such an extreme in which the account is force-liquidated by the brokerage firm, he will no longer have the luxury of picking a price. Instead, the "margin man" will simply begin offsetting positions regardless of price, liquidity, and so on. Unfortunately, Murphy's Law seems to run rampant in these situations; ironically, traders have an inclination to run out of money or margin at the absolute worst time. I can't tell you how many force-liquidated accounts are required to live through the agony of watching the market move favorably just after being forced out of positions by their brokerage firm's risk management department. The same traders also have a tendency to blame their broker for the ill-timed liquidation, but in reality they should blame themselves for putting their brokerage in that situation in the first place. The last thing brokerage firms want to do is interfere with client trading accounts. Forced liquidation is a last-ditch effort to gain control over the risk posed by the client, and if put in that situation the outcome is the trader's "doing," not the brokerage firm's.

Aside from leverage and possible premature forced-liquidation, lightly capitalized futures accounts might not have the means to hold positions overnight when necessary due to

> "Time is your friend; impulse is your enemy." —Jack Bogle

the higher margin rates that come with holding positions beyond the close. CME currency futures close at 4:00 p.m. Central, but that doesn't mean your technical setup has had a chance to play itself out. It might be crucial to hold positions into the overnight session, or even the next trading day, to give your strategy a fair chance to succeed. It is a good idea to keep extra money on deposit to ensure the ability to hold a position for multiple sessions if necessary, even if that wasn't the original intention. Don't forget, FOREX currency traders face the same margin requirement for day trading as they do position trading.

Trade Less to Make More

Often to their own detriment, those drawn to short-term currency trading tend to have hyperactive personalities, and this often affects trading results in a dramatically negative way. We are all human, and we all experience bouts of greed, but to be a successful trader it is imperative to come to the realization that less is often more. We all know that trading is theoretically a zero-sum game in which there is a winner for every loser; therefore, the *only* way to come out ahead is to consistently put the odds in your favor. In essence, this simply means patiently waiting for either good (or better yet, great) opportunities. Unfortunately, rather than exercising patience, many inexperienced traders force execution out of boredom; if they don't lose money in the market, they end up with a hefty commission bill that eats away at their trading account…and yes, this is even true if you are trading so called "commission-free" FOREX.

Most people look at being flat the market as a missed opportunity, but I encourage them to see it in the opposite light. If you are on the sidelines, you aren't losing money; also, you will be in a much better position to take advantage

> In trading, one person's misery is another person's joy.

of a promising opportunity should it come along. Dr. Mohamed A. El-Erian, CEO of one of the largest bond funds in the world, once touted that people often overlook the value of the "optionality" of holding cash on the sidelines. He believes that doing so puts investors in a position to capitalize on the abnormal opportunities that can suddenly arise.

You should be asking yourself, "How do I know when an opportunity is promising?" The answer to this question will depend on your strategy (trend following, scalping, and so on), but in my opinion, as discussed in Chapter 12, "Getting Technical with Currencies," countertrend trading might be the most appealing. In the end, if the goal is to buy low and sell high, shouldn't you be looking to go long a currency when it appears to be "cheap" relative to its recent history? This is in opposition to buying it after it has already gone up enough to trigger a signal for you, and everyone else, to go long. Remember, most traders lose money, so you typically don't want to be following the masses.

Are Protective Stops Really "Protective"?

As a reminder, a **stop order** is an instruction to execute a trade at the best possible price if the market moves unfavorably enough to reach a stated price. This is the exact opposite of a limit order, which is an attempt to buy or sell at a better price than is currently available. A stop order, unbelievably, is an order to buy or sell at a *worse* price. Specifically, a stop order is an order to buy or sell a currency pair, or a currency futures contract, once the price of the instrument reaches a specified level, at which time it becomes a market order. For this reason, this is one order type that most traders hope is never filled.

Stop orders can be used to enter a market, but most traders use it as a means of exiting. You've probably heard this referred to as a "stop loss order" because it is viewed as a protective measure to stop losses beyond a specified price point. I would venture to say most trading books and courses preach that traders should *always* use stop loss orders. The theory behind this is that stop orders will prevent losses from running out of control and will work toward eliminating some of the psychological anguish involved in picking an exit point of a losing trade.

However, for those using low, or at least reasonable, levels of leverage, I am not convinced that stop loss orders are the best method of risk management. In fact, in my opinion, the use of stop orders often increase the odds of trading failure. Anybody who has experienced a stop loss being filled just before the market reverses understands the emotional turmoil it can cause. Not only was that particular trade a failure, but it can have a negative impact on trader psychology going forward, and could affect future trades as well.

Based on my observations, stop loss orders *make* more money for brokerage firms than they *save* traders. This is partly because traders who have just been stopped out of a position often re-establish the trade nearly immediately; they justify their actions by claiming their stop was run by the broker or market maker and was triggered by a temporary price move. Most forget that a stop loss can only do its job if you walk away once it is placed or at least accept it once it is filled.

With that said, I question whether the purpose a stop order serves traders is a worthy one. If the goal is to buy low and sell high, by definition, a stop order is going to be an antagonist to what a trader is trying to accomplish. Remember, a stop order is executed only if the price gets *worse*.

> "Intellectual capital will always trump financial capital."
> —Paul Tudor Jones

Also, stop loss orders have a strong propensity to be filled. The explanation might simply be that market makers (or the "smart money") are gunning for stops, that most traders place their stop orders too close to the current price, or perhaps that the markets, and speculating in them, is a cruel joke being played on retail traders. In any case, traders placing stop loss orders should assume the odds favor a fill.

Those placing stop loss orders too close to the action aren't properly compensating for natural price fluctuations and are prone to suffer small and frequent losses with little chance of surviving trades long enough to see their hard work and risk pay off. On the other hand, traders placing their stop loss at distant prices will potentially suffer substantial losses, and Murphy's Law suggests that it's likely the market will reverse just after reaching the trader's stop loss order.

I am not sure which scenario is most agonizing, but there might be a solution that is much less painful—namely, options. Although it is beyond the scope of this text, I feel compelled to make mention of the fact that options can be purchased as a form of insurance against incorrect speculation in the underlying currency. Doing so avoids the complications of placing traditional stop loss orders as a means of risk management. Of course, nothing in life is free, and if you want to limit your risk via an insurance (purchased call or put), it is going to cost you.

Give Yourself a Chance!

Some traders aren't mentally capable of trading without stops, and even those convinced they are can find themselves guilty of letting a loser get out of hand. Placing a stop order enables traders to avoid the extreme grief associated with manually admitting they were wrong and pulling the plug on a trade—and this can be difficult to do. Also, the use of stop orders means traders can conduct their analysis, enter the trade, place their exit orders on both the profitable (limit) and losing (stop) side of the market, and walk away. For some, the ability to walk away from the stress of seeing the outcome is necessary to control the flurry of sometimes harmful emotions that come with having hard-earned money in the markets.

For those who "must" use stop orders, it is critical they give themselves an opportunity to make money. For instance, traders should be aware of their projected win/loss ratio and place stop orders accordingly. A trader who averages a losing trade for every winning trade would have very little chance of trading successfully if he placed equal profit targets and stop losses. Doing so would mean any gains would be offset by the corresponding losses—and that is before considering commission or fees paid to the brokerage firm. In other words, not only would it be nearly impossible for such a strategy to be profitable based on market gains and losses, the

> The market never sleeps, but it can't tell time either. Make sure you are giving your strategy ample time to produce results!

additional transaction costs make the probabilities even worse, maybe even impossible.

On the other hand, a trend trader might make money on 30% of his trades and lose on 70%. This might sound extremely unappealing, but that is the reality of a trend-trading method. As discussed in Chapter 12, such a strategy is built on the premise that although markets spend most of the time range bound, causing frequent losses, once a strong trend emerges, the profit on the few winning trades could be enormous enough to offset the losers...plus some.

In either instance, those using stop orders should not place their stop deeper than the profit target on a percentage basis. If you are risking more than you stand to make, your win/loss ratio would need to be considerably higher than 50%. Regrettably, when it comes to futures or FX trading, a high percentage of winners relative to losers isn't likely. Most traders strive for a win/loss ratio of 50%.

> "It's not whether you're right or wrong that's important, but how much money you make when you're right and how much you lose when you're wrong."
> —George Soros

On a side note, if you are familiar with option trading (particularly option selling), you likely know the win/loss ratios are much different. In fact, short option traders might make money on 70% to 80% of their trades, but it is the 20% or 30% that lose that can really wreak havoc on a trading account. Option buyers face the exact opposite stats. Despite the known challenges, I happen to be an advocate of option selling. If you have an interest in learning more about options, option spreads, and option selling, you might find my book *Commodity Options,* published by FT Press, a helpful source of information.

Position Sizing

A common mistake among beginning traders is to take on too much leverage; in this day and age of technology, buying or selling multiple contracts is as simple as clicking a button. Accordingly, I would venture to say that most day traders execute quantities in excess of what is ideal based on available capital. In my opinion, even traders who are within the parameters of the minimum margin requirements are likely biting off more than they can chew.

As a Las Vegas local, I know all about the gluttonous nature of humans. Excessive leverage taken on by traders is similar to buffet patrons enjoying three or four desserts. It might be easily accessible and free, but in the end it isn't good for anyone.

Although human nature and greed play a big part in the overleveraging of traders, it isn't all their fault. Brokerage firms are partly to blame for extending highly discounted margins to futures day traders and marketing high-leveraged trading as an attraction to the FOREX market. Nonetheless, in the end it is the trader's choice whether to use it just as it is the buffet patron's prerogative to limit him or herself to single servings.

The number of contracts traded at a time should be based on personal risk tolerance and the amount of available capital. The truth is, we are all wired differently and it is imperative to avoid pushing yourself beyond (or even to) the limits of your trading comfort zone. Traders who are putting money at risk they can't afford to lose, or are establishing positions that are well beyond their tolerance level, will be trading with "scared money." Scared traders are prone to panicked decision making; this is typically associated with poor timing and illogical trading practices.

Once again, the NFA prohibits FX brokers from offering leverage higher than 50 to 1. However, as a rule of thumb, I recommend traders avoid using leverage in excess of 10 to 1 and perhaps, ideally, closer to 5 to 1 in many cases. In a nutshell, this equates to holding $10,000 in capital for $100,000 in nominal value of a currency pair. Of course, you can easily fit five times the trading size in a $10,000 account, but just because you can doesn't mean you should (think Las Vegas buffet and desserts).

I realize this sounds incredibly boring; if you are taking the time to read this book, you have likely already been exposed to the idea of the super-charged profits that leverage can provide to traders. Nevertheless, highly leveraged traders are much more liable to suffer large losses than they are to celebrate trading profits taking them into the next tax bracket. Instead of placing large wagers on low-probability trades looking for life-changing profits, why not slow things down and favorably shift the odds of success?

Look at it this way: An average profit of $50 per day equates to $1,000 per month, assuming 20 trading days. In a year's time, $50 per day becomes $12,000. If a trader was skilled enough to produce $50 in profits each day after deducting commission (if any is charged), she would more than double a $10,000 account in a year. In fact, a net of $50 per day would produce a profit of 120% per year on an account with the stated beginning account balance. To put this into perspective, the top CTAs (Commodity Trading Advisors) and hedge funds in the country struggle to net a return of 20% to 30% per year. For a second time, the infamous Bernie Madoff fund was only yielding 13% annually—and investors were flocking to participate in what turned out to be a history-making Ponzi scheme.

The point I am trying to make is that traders must be realistic in what is, and isn't, possible. Although tales of traders doubling or tripling accounts in a matter of days or months exist, it should be considered the equivalent of hitting the lottery. It can happen, but isn't likely. More importantly, it does not take ten standard lots in FX, or ten currency futures, to make $50 per day, but I believe that attempting to trade such size will dramatically increase the odds of a trader blowing out the account (losing everything), while simultaneously padding the pockets of the brokerage firm.

Price Averaging

One of the most common concepts of risk management is centered around the mantra "don't add to losers." However, for those with well-capitalized accounts I believe adding to a position as a means of adjusting your breakeven price makes sense. After all, if you liked it at yesterday's price and today's is even better, why not improve your average entry price?

With that said, adding to losing positions is something that should be done with care and isn't an excuse to completely disregard our desire to keep leverage well within the set limits. In other words, adding to a losing position doesn't mean executing a EUR/USD pair every 10 pips. Only the trader himself will know what the

There are two types of losses: money and opportunity!

comfortable and appropriate intervals will be and how many contracts to add to a position. For example, an aggressive short-term intraday trader practicing a strategy that includes a profit target of 20 pips might indeed be comfortable adding a contract on 5 or 10 pips of unfavorable price movement. Conversely, a position trader attempting to catch a move of 300 or 400 pips might only want to add a contract in the scenario of an adverse 200-pip price move.

> Momentum traders look to buy currencies after they have already rallied significantly and sell currencies that are in a bear market. However, more often than not this will lead to the exact opposite of the intention to buy low and sell high!

Once a contract is added at a "better" price, the trader's entry is averaged to a more favorable level and therefore the market has to retrace less to return a profit. Simply adding to a losing position shifts the breakeven point of the trade to a price that is more easily attainable. Naturally, there is a drawback—adding to a loser is equivalent to doubling down, or more if you add several contracts. Accordingly, the opportunity cost of adding positions to better the breakeven point is that traders are simultaneously increasing the risk, and magnifying losses, should the market continue to move adversely.

Another aspect of price averaging that must be realized is that for those trading standard FX contracts (100,000 units) or the full-sized futures contracts, it could take a sizable trading account and nerves of steel to practice a strategy that involves adding risk to losers. However, in both trading arenas, smaller contracts are available to enable moderately funded trading accounts to participate in such a strategy.

Price Averaging with E-micro Futures

I believe those looking to hold long or short speculative trades for longer periods of time might be best off approaching the market with a scaled trading strategy stripped of some of the leverage in trading standard FX and currency futures contracts. In my belief, the most efficient manner of doing this might involve the use of the CME Group's relatively newly listed Micro FX futures contracts, which present traders with a relatively low-leveraged alternative to currency speculation.

Because of the exchange guarantee provided by futures exchanges, along with heavy regulation, and a lack of broker conflict of interest, I chose to focus on using the CME Group's currency futures products. However, similar strategies could be executed with the use of FX mini lots, or even FX micro pairs. Keep in mind that there is a confusing discrepancy between futures and FX lingo; FX micro pairs are based on 1,000 units of currency whereas the futures E-micros are based on either 10,000 or 12,500, depending on the contract. In other words, the E-micro in futures is *not* similarly sized to the micro in FX; instead, the E-micro is nearly equivalent to the mini lot in FX.

> "A handful of patience is worth more than a bushel of brains."
> —Dutch proverb

The CME Group launched its E-micro FOREX futures in answer to the micro lots offered in FOREX that were attracting an entirely new type of speculator—the one who wants to trade with less than $1,000 and fund his account with a credit card. Although you will likely never be able to fund a futures account with a credit card, nor would I advocate it (leverage on leverage never ends well), the E-micro FOREX futures at the CME Group are 1/10th the size of the standard contract and offer futures traders the same low-margined opportunity. Smaller contract size translates into 1/10th of the risk exposure and position volatility.

Along with tamer profits and losses comes a lower margin rate. The EUR/USD E-micro futures carries the largest margin requirement at a rate of about $430, and the USD/CHF E-micro involves the lowest at about $206. I am not necessarily advising that you open a trading account with $300 dollars and roll the dice. What I *am* saying is that E-micros might be a great opportunity for moderately funded accounts to establish relatively long-term currency positions with the luxury of scaling in and out of the trade.

Despite the fact that currency trading has a tendency to lure day traders, expectedly due to high leverage ratio (it's probably hard to sleep when holding positions with leverage of 50 to 1 or higher), there are opportunities for position trading as well.

Nobody has a crystal ball to tell them where the Euro will be trading versus the U.S. Dollar at any point in the future, but we don't need a crystal ball to tell us that currencies have historically had a tendency to trade within a range. Although there are no guarantees the Euro can't go above $1.6000 to make new all-time highs, a bearish trader speculating with a time frame of a month or two might deem that the odds seem to be against it.

Perhaps Euro prices within the vicinity of all-time highs would be an attractive place for a bearish scale trade. Assuming the Euro is trading at $1.4800, E-micro futures traders would presumably have the wherewithal to withstand the pain of new all-time highs. For instance, a move from $1.4800 to $1.6000 in an E-micro Euro is equivalent to $1,500 profit or loss to the trader. Accordingly, a moderately funded account might be able to stomach the risk of trading one lot from the short side, and even adding contracts on every 300 or 400 points. Doing so shifts the breakeven point on the trade to a higher, more realistic level (the higher the average entry price, the less the market has to drop for the trader to profit).

Remember, an E-micro is 1/10th of the standard contract, so a trader can sell a total of ten contracts on the way up (at better prices) before reaching the same leverage and risk of a standard contract. Of course, the downside of this strategy is when the market drops (assuming it does) without the trader having an opportunity to sell all ten (or whatever the desired leverage and risk amount is); however, is that really such a horrible outcome? After all, the trader was right and was making money—I can think of much worse scenarios.

Naturally, it would likely be wise to peel off contracts at various prices should the market turn in your favor. If you scale into a trade, it is often best to scale out of it too.

High-Frequency Trading in Currencies

In recent years, and especially in the wake of the infamous equity market flash crash, much criticism has fallen on the practice of what is collectively known as high-frequency trading (HFT). HFT is defined as program trading that utilizes powerful computers to transact multiple orders at very fast speeds. Trades are executed via complex algorithms that attempt to predict price movement, but many argue the speed and resiliency of HFT programs drive prices to much further extremes than what would otherwise be the case…and they are probably right.

High-frequency trading has certainly impacted the markets and the way prices fluctuate. For instance, in many cases the added liquidity could mean better fill quality, but in other circumstances it might mean larger price swings. Humans have a tendency to look at change in a negative context; however, I'm not convinced the overall impact of HFT is either positive or negative—just different. Personally, I believe traders should focus on how and where the market is going rather than why or how it is getting there.

> We can't direct the wind, but we can adjust the sails.

Traders are, in essence, competing with all other market participants—whether it be an algo-trading system, a specialist on the trading floor, or someone clicking a mouse in their pajamas. In my opinion, it is naive to assume that it is possible to completely level the playing field. Even if high-frequency traders were banned from the marketplace, there will usually be somebody, or some entity, who will have more resources and knowledge than you. For instance, Warren Buffet isn't a high-frequency trader but he certainly has the means to conduct fundamental research better than the rest of us. Similarly, someone standing on the floor of the CME (Chicago Mercantile Exchange) or the CBOE (Chicago Board of Exchange) will probably have some sort of informational advantage.

In previous decades, traders standing in the currency futures pits on the floor of the CME had the undeniable advantage; unfortunately for them, that is no longer the case. As markets have moved toward electronic and over-the-counter trading, the "edge" has simply shifted away from floor brokers/market makers and toward high-frequency traders; once again, I don't believe the market is any better or worse off, it is just different… and investors must learn to adjust accordingly.

Risk Capital Only

Although some traders have found ways to successfully make a living trading currencies, there are far more who join the masses to become a statistic. It is easy to be lured into the dream of trading for a living; in spite of everything, trading doesn't seem like work—you can write your own schedule and call in sick anytime you feel like it. Similarly,

FOREX system software and education vendors make it come across as if trading profitably is easy. In some cases, they claim it is as simple as buying when a platform gives you a green flashing light and selling when it turns red. How could anything go wrong?

Alas, anything that seems too good to be true usually is. Certainly a massive amount of money is up for grabs in the financial markets each day, and based on the laws of trading, there is a winner for every loser. Nevertheless, we now know the odds of success are far less than 50%, despite this.

If you walk away from this book with the understanding of one concept, I hope it is this: Regardless of your intentions in speculation or your chosen market, there is one common rule—never trade with money you can't afford to lose. If you are like me, it seems like there is no such thing as money that can be lost without some type of anguish. Nonetheless, risk capital is defined as an amount of money that, if lost, would not alter your current lifestyle. Specifically, if the money deposited in a trading account will affect the funding of your children's education, your ability to put food on the table, or even dictate your overall quality of life, you have no business participating in the markets.

Conclusion

I've always believed that you get out of life what you put into it; trading currencies is no different. Traders will ultimately determine their fate in the markets by the manner in which they approach them. If the goal is an adrenaline rush, there are plenty to be had and free highly leveraged instruments for the taking. For those looking to turn a few thousand dollars into millions without breaking a sweat, they can sure give it a try, but might have more luck playing the state lottery. On the other hand, for those who have brushed aside dreams of getting rich quick and are satisfied with meeting their craving for excitement with an energy drink rather than the financial markets, the potential for conservative yet attractive, returns is at their fingertips.

The reality is, successful currency trading in futures, FX, or ETFs requires a tremendous amount of research, well-tuned discipline, and instinct. Not only do traders need education and experience to accurately predict market price, but they must be aware of the intricacies of the market that are unique to currencies, such as the FX carry trade, dealing desks, and currency futures rollovers.

In addition to these basic skills and knowledge, traders seeking success in the currency markets must be willing to treat leverage with care. I would venture to say that most profitable currency traders dilute leverage by funding their trading account with more than the minimum margin requirement. In any case, it is up to the trader to determine her comfort level, strengths, and weaknesses. Unfortunately, these are realizations that only come with experience. Good luck!

14

Currency Lingo

lthough my goal is to make this book as least academic as possible, I recognize that currency traders have a language all their own. Accordingly, before it is possible to fully understand the mechanics of the FOREX and futures markets, let alone the theories that drive prices, taking the time to learn the "industry tongue" is a necessary evil.

By nature, traders and those that surround themselves with the markets (brokers, money managers, and so on) tend to be highly organized and efficient, but they are also somewhat creative. As we have touched upon, retail FX brokerage firms ran aggressive (and borderline genius) marketing campaigns prior to government regulatory intervention. When I use the word "genius," I'm implying clever gimmicks, not necessarily integrity in their efforts. Although there were, and are, honest and trustworthy FOREX brokers and brokerage firms, as with most things in life, there were some bad apples that gave the others a bad name. Nonetheless, if you are interested in trading currencies and would like to be able to communicate efficiently with your broker, your buddies, or even your spouse (trust me, most spouses aren't keen on risking the family money in the markets, and you will need all the help you can get), you had better be prepared.

Here are several terms you will most likely run into during your travels, and throughout this text. Some are simply slang used in the back rooms of brokerage firms everywhere, and others are words you would hear on a business news station. Either way, you owe it to yourself to be aware of their meaning and implication.

Pip

The smallest unit of price movement in a foreign currency; a pip is equivalent to a cent in stock trading or a tick in futures trading. In most trading platforms and in most currency pairs, it will be the fourth digit to the right of the decimal point. For example, if the EUR/USD goes from 1.4235 to 1.4236, it has moved 1 pip. The Japanese Yen is an exception to the rule; if the USD/JPY falls from 79.03 to 79.02, it has dropped 1 pip.

Pip Spread

The difference between the best available bid and the best available ask (discussed in detail in Chapter 5, "FOREX Trading Quotes and Calculations").

Bid

The price at which a retail trader can sell. In turn, it is the best price counterparties are willing to buy. In other words, the bid price shown in a trading platform represents the working buy limit orders of other traders or market makers. In the case of the bid, the "best" price is the highest price because retail traders must sell the bid, and selling at a higher price is favorable.

Ask

The ask price is the one at which a retail trader can buy; conversely, it is the best price (lowest) counterparties are willing to sell. The ask price displayed in a trading platform represents the best working limit order placed by others to sell. The "best" price for a retail trader is the lowest price when it comes to the ask, which is the opposite of the bid.

Offer

In FX, futures, and even stocks, the offer price is the current ask price. It is commonly referred to as the offer because it is the best available price at which a counterparty is willing to sell. In other words, the counterparty is "offering" to sell at the ask price. Ask and offer are synonyms and can be used interchangeably.

Big Figure Quote

The non-pip portion of the price quote, or the first few digits of an exchange rate; in futures this is com-monly referred to as a "handle." The easiest way to look at it is the "big figure" portion of the price quote is the stem or whole dollar price of a quote. For example, if the USD/CAD is bid at 0.9675 and the ask is 0.9677, the big figure quote is .96. Accordingly, brokers and traders might drop the big figure quote altogether and verbally refer to the current price as 75 bid, 77 offered. You might also hear someone say, "75 bid at 77," or even "75 at 77."

Ballooning of Pips

Ballooning is the practice of dealers widening the spread between bids and asks in FOREX during highly volatile or illiquid market conditions. For those participating in a true market (futures or an ECN) in which the bids and asks float based on current liquidity and price transparency of all market participants, this is less of a concern. However, it still occurs as market makers attempt to protect themselves from the unnecessary risks of providing liquidity services in certain market conditions.

I encourage traders to expect spread widening around economic releases that have a tendency to receive violent market reactions and adjust their trading strategy accordingly. Such events include, but are not limited to, the government's monthly employment report and Federal Open Market Committee (FOMC) meetings. That said, if you are trading with a non-ECN broker/dealing desk that seems to take ballooning of spreads beyond risk management and to a point where it is consistently putting your ability, as a client, to execute trades at fair prices behind profit potential, it is time to look for a new broker. Once again, if you have a tendency to be a conspiracy theorist, you will be best off going with an ECN or futures account. The added stress of questioning the ethics of your broker could easily affect trading results.

Stop Harvesting/Price Spiking

Stop harvesting, or price spiking, is the practice of dealing desks (non-ECN brokers) pushing market prices to trigger working stop orders. Obviously, this is a detriment to clients but an advantage to the counterparty on the other side of the trade (in this case, the dealing desk). This practice is difficult to prove and is aggressively denied by brokerage firms. Nonetheless, clients often feel otherwise.

Requoting

A requote occurs when a client is filled at a price not displayed in the trading platform. A client who clicks the green button on an FX trading pad to buy a currency pair at the ask typically expects the fill to be reported at the price displayed. However, it is conceivable that the ask changed in the split-second the client's finger pressed the button on his mouse, but in a requote the fill might be reported a few pips higher than the displayed price. Requoting occurs only if you are trading with a market maker, or non-ECN broker, but is quickly becoming a thing of the past thanks to NFA regulations honing in on the practice. Keep in mind that such an occurrence is not, and has never been, acceptable in electronically executed futures trading. That said, data feeds and computer software are not perfect, so in some cases clients might feel as though they are victims of a requote, or something similar, when instead it was a technical failure.

Over the Counter

This term is used to describe any transaction that does not take place in a centralized location such as an exchange floor. In the case of stock trading, the NASDAQ is the most famous over-the-counter market, but in FX all transactions are over the counter simply because there is no exchange. This is true regardless of brokerage type.

Off-Exchange Currency Trading

Perhaps in an effort for regulators such as the NFA and the CFTC to emphasize the fact that FOREX transactions do not take place on an organized (and regulated) exchange, they have dubbed currency trading in FX as "off-exchange." Not surprisingly, currency futures, which are traded on an exchange (primarily the CME) are referred to as "on-exchange."

Liquidity Provider

Typically, a liquidity provider is a bank or similar entity that feeds bid and ask prices to brokerage firms, to ultimately be viewed within the trading platforms of brokerage clients. Many ECN brokers offer access to networks in which multiple liquidity providers are present.

ECN (Electronic Communications Network)

An ECN is a system in which the buy and sell orders of retail clients are routed to a network of banks and dealers who act as market makers by serving as the counterparty to client trades. In the vast world of FOREX, there are several ECNs, and not all ECNs are created equal. In general, the bigger the ECN, the more liquidity provided to traders and the better the fill quality.

The ECN only exists in FX; futures traders enjoy similar networks facilitated by futures exchanges, but they fall under various names. CME Group currency futures trade on a single network known simply as GLOBEX.

Trading Lots and Contract Size

When I refer to "lots," I am not talking about plenty. Instead, I am referring to the particular unit of measure used to quantify the number of contracts in futures, or nominal size in FX. The use of the word "lot" in futures is a little easier to comprehend. A futures "lot" is simply a contract; accordingly, a trader who is said to be trading five lots is trading five contracts. If the trader doesn't specify whether he is trading a mini, E-micro, or standard contract, it is typically safe to assume he is referring to a standard contract (most standard currency futures are 125,000 to 100,000 units).

Although you will sometimes hear FX traders using the same word, it can mean different things to different to different traders. In general, if a FOREX trader claims to be trading one lot, he is trading the standard 100,000 units. However, it isn't uncommon for those trading mini FX or micro FX lots to fail to specify. I guess you can't blame them; it's much more impressive to let people assume you are trading 100,000 units than to admit you are trading 1,000 units and making or losing about a dime per pip.

FOREX industry insiders, on the other hand, often skip the word "lot" and simply specify the size of the order. This is because FX trading is much easier to customize relative to futures when it comes to trading size. Futures traders can choose between standard, mini, and E-micro contracts and then execute trades according to the number of lots desired in each size. FX traders, on the other hand, can easily trade in increments of 10,000, ranging from 10,000 to 1,000,000, by simply stipulating the size of the trade within their platforms.

FCM

Futures Commission Merchant (FCM) is a futures registration category with the NFA that grants the firm the ability to collect client money for trading purposes along with soliciting clients and accepting orders to buy or sell futures and FX contracts. FCMs are responsible for housing client funds, issuing account statements, and seeing that each trade is properly cleared with the futures exchange (if applicable).

Dealer

In contrast to a traditional broker who simply matches buyers and sellers, a dealer is an individual or firm that takes it a step further by acting as a principal or counterparty to client transaction. In essence, a dealer is hoping to take the opposite side of one trader's execution and later closing the position in a subsequent trade with another party in hopes of profiting from the pip spread between the bid and the ask. In general, the dealers aren't interested in speculating on price movement or accepting risk exposure of price movement, although sometimes they do (and are). Instead, in accordance with their market making, if there isn't another retail order enabling them to offset their risk immediately, they will often execute an opposite transaction in the interbank market as a means of maintaining balance on their books. In other words, they work to keep the balance of all their positions acquired through market-making essentially flat with the market. Therefore, for every long 100,000 of EUR/USD, they want to be short 100,000 somewhere else.

Introducing Broker

Introducing brokers are commonly referred to as IBs and comprise a registration category with the NFA (National Futures Association). An introducing broker is a person or entity that acquires brokerage clients for a much larger broker that either acts as a dealer or can provide access to the ECN markets. In futures trading, introducing brokers must be affiliated with an FCM (Futures Commission Merchant) to acquire exchange clearing services for their clients. In FOREX, they might be affiliated with an RFED (Retail Foreign Exchange Dealer) rather than an FCM.

In its simplest form, an introducing broker is a broker working for a larger brokerage entity who is paid as a contractor (on a 1099 basis) as opposed to an employee (on a W-2 basis).

Retail Foreign Exchange Dealer (RFED)

An NFA registration category for brokerage firms that act as a counterparty to off-exchange currency traders but do not offer trading of on-exchange products (futures).

FOREX Dealer Member

An NFA registration category that includes firms that offer on-exchange futures products but are also engaged in off-exchange currency activities in which they act as the counterparty.

Associated Person (AP)

Another NFA registration category used to describe an individual broker. An AP is an individual who solicits orders, customers, and customer funds on behalf of an FCM or IB.

Clearing

Clearing is the procedure by which an organization acts as an intermediary to the buyer and seller in a futures transaction. The goal is to reconcile orders, or simply match buys and sells, between transacting parties. Clearing enables markets to be highly efficient because it eliminates the need to transfer contracts between each individual party; instead, each party is transacting with the clearinghouse itself.

Each futures exchange has its own clearinghouse. At the end of each trading day, all exchange members (mostly brokerage firms) are required to deposit a specific sum of money with the clearinghouse based on the outstanding margin requirement.

The brokerage is responsible for only the net margin requirement, not the total. For instance, if a firm's clients are holding 125,000 long positions in the December Euro, but client accounts are also holding 100,000 short the Euro, the broker is only required to deposit the margin on 25,000 contracts.

Going Short

The sale of an asset or contract (liability) with the premise of falling prices. "Going short" is also called "shorting a market." Price declines enable short traders to buy the asset back at a lower price at some point to realize a profit. If a trader must (or chooses to) buy the contract back at a higher price, a loss is realized.

Going Long

The purchase of a speculative instrument with the intentions of it appreciating in value to enable the trader to sell, or offset the position, at a higher price.

Currency Cross or Cross-Currency Pair

A cross-currency is one in which the trader's domestic currency is not a component to the pair. Assuming the U.S. Dollar is the trader's home currency, examples of a currency cross are the EUR/GBP and the AUD/CAD. You might also hear the term "cross-rate." This is simply the quote of any cross-currency pair. Trading cross-currencies, as well as non-cross-currencies, in which the U.S. Dollar is not the quote currency (USD/JPY, for example) requires converting the profit or loss in pips into terms of the quote currency and then converting that amount into the trader's home currency.

Loonie or Canuck Buck

If you ever hear a currency trader talk about the Loonie (not loony), don't be offended; she is probably not insulting you. The Loonie is a slang term for the Canadian Dollar. Another relatively commonly used nickname for the Canadian is the Canuck Buck.

Swissy

This one seems rather obvious, but at the same time, I couldn't leave it out. FX traders often refer to the Swiss Franc as the "Swissy." In addition, although there are other Francs, the Swiss Franc is considered to be *The* Franc.

Kiwi

Kiwi is slang for the New Zealand Dollar. The New Zealand Dollar is not among the uber-liquid within the FX complex. Therefore, I believe it should be traded sparingly. Nonetheless, if you hear Kiwi at a FOREX event, you'll know they aren't talking about fruit.

Cable

FX traders often refer to the GBP/USD pair as the "cable." This label was derived from the fact that in the mid-1800s the price quote was transmitted via a transatlantic cable. The name has stuck, even in today's Internet and computer environment.

Book

A trader's or broker's "book" has nothing to do with paper, typed text, and a cover, or even a Kindle or Nook; in the world of trading a "book" refers to the combined total positions or cumulative capital. For instance, an FX broker with a substantial number of clients, or maybe a few clients with substantial funding, might brag about the size of his book. On the other hand, the dealing desk is constantly monitoring its book to determine its net position and risk. To illustrate, if its clients are net long 1,000,000 worth of the EUR/USD, it would likely want to take an opposite position in the FX market to ensure it isn't exposed to substantial price risk.

High-Frequency Trading

As the name implies, high-frequency trading consists of aggressive and active trading, which typically falls into the scalping category. High-frequency trading is almost always executed via automated computer programs or algorithmic trading systems in which specific mathematical code is written to react to certain market events. In the case of high-frequency trading, there is little human involvement. As the computers take over, there is the possibility of extreme price movement. For instance, many believe that algorithmic trading was at least partly responsible for the infamous flash crash in U.S. equities on May 6, 2010. You might also hear this practice referred to as program trading or algo (algorithmic) trading.

P&L

Profit and loss is rarely depicted in statements and platforms by its full name. In other words, if you ever see these letters without additional explanation, it is fair to say that they are in reference to profit and loss.

Bank Rate

FX traders often speak about the "bank rate." By definition, this is the rate at which a central bank lends money to banks within its domestic banking system. In the U.S., this is referred to as the "Federal Discount rate."

Exotics

Despite the name, exotic currency pairs are not those that represent tropical countries...although they might be. Exotic currency pairs involve either the USD or the EUR paired against emerging economies.

Examples of exotics are the USD/TRY (Dollar versus Turkish Lira) and the USD/SGD (U.S. Dollar versus Singapore Dollar).

Exotic currencies tend to be far less liquid than the majors and therefore aren't recommended for beginning traders; in addition, such currency pairs tend to be more at risk of dramatic price moves due to political unrest.

EA (Expert Advisor)/Automated Trading Systems

Expert Advisor (EA) is a term used specifically in FOREX trading; although similar products exist in futures, they are not referred to as EAs but rather as automated trading systems, or algo-trading. An EA is preprogrammed software that facilitates automated pairs trading in FX. Specifically, EAs execute buy and sell orders according to specific technical indicators and mathematical occurrences.

EAs essentially remove the emotional turmoil of deciding when to enter and exit the market by simply executing orders on behalf of the trader according to predesigned trading systems. For instance, some EAs might open a position based on signals triggered in indicators such as the Relative Strength Index (RSI), Stochastics, and the Average Directional Index (ADX), or a combination of all three (or more). In other words, EAs are prepackaged trading systems that are intended to do all the work for the trader and remove the emotional and logistic challenges from choosing and executing trades. However, I caution you that as good as this sounds, in most cases it can be chalked up as one of those "too good to be true" scenarios.

EAs, or simply automated trading systems for futures traders, can typically be purchased or leased, and they are not cheap. Some firms offer packages for which traders will be provided software or code for several systems for one lump sum (usually several thousand), and other firms offer monthly or quarterly leases running anywhere from a few hundred to several hundred per month. Clearly, anybody using a trading system or EA has some hurdles to overcome. The trading method itself would have to be profitable enough to cover any transaction costs incurred, as well as the cost of the system, for the trader to reap any of the reward. Unfortunately, system vendors and sales people aren't always as diligent in pointing this out; don't let yourself be fooled by track records published by entities not registered with the NFA. NFA registrants are required to follow strict regulations and are regularly audited, but non-NFA firms have

been known to exercise their right to freedom of speech a little too freely. Triple-digit annual returns published by venders are sometimes the result of creative math—or smoke and mirrors.

Flat or Square

If a trader is said to be "flat" or "square," he does not currently have any open positions. In other words, being square with the market means there is no risk exposure or obligations with the exchange, a broker, or any other counterparty.

Gap

A price gap occurs if the price of a currency pair or currency future changes from the close of one session to the open of another. In FOREX, the end of the trading day is considered to be 5:00 p.m. Eastern, but during the trading week there is no pause in trading and therefore no potential for a price gap. Futures traded on the CME, on the other hand, are closed for 1 hour per day; from 4:00 p.m. to 5:00 p.m. Central time during the trading week. Although not necessarily common, it is entirely possible for a currency futures contract to see a significant price change on the 5:00 open relative to the 4:00 close. This tends to be a relatively uneventful time of day, which is why the CME chooses this as its closing hour. After all, at that time the U.S. markets are closed and the Asian markets have yet to open; nonetheless, gaps are possible.

The most likely time for price gaps in either FOREX or currency futures is over the weekend. As you can imagine, substantial political and economic events or realizations could take place between the Friday evening close and the Sunday evening open. Accordingly, is possible to see substantial price gaps as the financial markets open up to start the week.

Jobber

A relatively aggressive day trader with particularly short time horizons. Jobbers are typically scalpers who execute comparatively large positions with extremely meager profit targets, typically 1 to 3 pips.

STP

STP (Straight Through Processing) doesn't require any manual intervention and is fully automatic. This simply means that your brokerage firm sets margin requirements to be levied by the trading platform, and orders placed are either automatically sent for execution or rejected based on the specific criteria. I would venture to say that all FX platforms and likely most stock and futures platforms are STP— although this wasn't the case just a few years ago. Obviously, STP enables traders faster and more effective execution, but it also means being rejected for a trade if your account is short the required margin by a few cents. Similarly, some platforms account for working orders when determining margin rather than only levying margin on open positions. If your broker's platform does this, you should probably look for another broker. Computers operate on math and are not capable of deciphering reason.

Swap/Rollover

A swap, or rollover, is the simultaneous purchase and sale of an identical amount of one currency for another with two different value dates (or delivery dates). Because FX contracts are agreements to make or take delivery two days into the future, it is necessary for positions that are held overnight (that is, by 5:00 p.m. Eastern) to be rolled over, or swapped, to avoid the delivery process. Fortunately for speculators, this practice is automatically done by FOREX brokerage firms.

Rollover/Carry Charges

Positions held beyond the NYC FOREX close not only must be rolled over, but they are also subject to an interest rate credit or charge. In essence, traders long the currency backed by the higher interest rate earn interest, or they pay interest if they are short the currency with a higher rate. We discuss this in detail in Chapter 3, "FX Brokers and the Reality of Transaction Costs."

Purchasing Power Parity (PPP)

Purchasing power parity is an economic theory dating back to the sixteenth century but developed into its modern form in 1918. According to PPP, exchange rates are based on the relative price levels of the two countries represented in the currency pair. In its simplest form, purchasing power parity assumes that identical goods will have the same price in both markets if expressed in a single currency. For years, economists have been comparing baskets of goods in relative countries, but the truth is that the purchasing power parity is extremely difficult to calculate because it is nearly impossible to find comparable baskets of goods and, naturally, different cultures. As a result, they will value items differently and or have various production and transportation costs. In other words, not only is PPP challenging to calculate but the number derived is likely somewhat useless anyway. Nonetheless, it is worth being aware of the concept because you will likely run across it as you research market fundamentals.

Index

Q–R

quotes

   currency, 17, 26, 36. *See also* currency

   pairs, 59

   pips, 61-63

   pricing, 60-61

   requoting, 32, 202

rates

   bank, 208

   commissions. *See* commissions

   interest, 135

   margins, 185

   money market, 36

ratios, Golden Ratio, 172

rebates, 38-40

recommendations, brokers, 41

Regular Stochastics, 167

regulations, 10

   NFA, 40-42. *See also* rules

Relative Strength Index (RSI), 165

reportable positions, 145

reports

   COT, 146-154

   traders, commitments of, 143-147

requirements, margins, 69

requoting, 32, 202

resources, seasonal trade, 156

Retail Foreign Exchange Dealer (RFED), 205

retail

   off-exchange currency mark, 5. *See also* FOREX

orders, 6. *See also* buying; selling

traders, excessive losses, 53

revenue, 29. *See also* costs

RFED (Retail Foreign Exchange Dealer), 205

risk

   accountability of, 72

   capital only, 196-197

   counterparty, 7, 129

   futures contracts, 68, 73

   interest rates, 135

   stop harvesting, 34

roll charges, 35, 38

rollovers, 36-37, 211

round turns, 39

RSI (Relative Strength Index), 165

rules

   CFTC, 52

   futures

     Aussie Dollars, 88

     British Pound, 89

     calculating, 83-85

     Canadian Dollars, 88

     Euro, 86

     Swiss Franc, 86

     Yen, 86-88

   no-hedging, 46-49

running stops, 34

S

seasonal trade cycles, 155-157

SEC (Securities and Exchange Commission), 143

secondary currency, 17

securities, 103

T

taxes, ETFs, 106-107
technical analysis, 159-160
  breakout traders, 161
  charting tools, 170-174
  countertrend traders, 161-162
  drawing channels/trend lines, 175-177
  indicators, 163-170
  oscillators, 163-170
  price gaps, 177-180
  technology, 162-163
  trend traders, 160
technology
  technical analysis, 162-163
  trading, 123
terminology
  AP, 205
  asks, 200
  bank rates, 208
  bids, 200
  big figure quotes, 201
  books, 207
  cable, 207
  carry charges, 211
  clearing, 205
  contract size, 203-204
  currency cross, 206
  dealers, 204
  EA, 209
  ECNs, 203
  exotics, 208
  FCM, 204
  flat, 210
  FOREX dealer members, 205
  HFT, 208
  introducing brokers, 205

jobbers, 211
Kiwi, 207
liquidity providers, 203
Loonies, 207
offers, 200
over the counter, 202
pips, 200-201
PPP, 212
pricing
  gaps, 210
  spiking, 201
requoting, 202
RFED, 205
rollovers, 211
square, 210
stop harvesting, 201
STP, 211
swaps, 211
Swissy, 207
trading, 203-204
theories, currency fundamental analysis, 134-138
ticker symbols, 23
timing
  GTC orders, 115
  limit orders, 112
  market orders, 110
  OCO orders, 114
  stop orders, 114
Tokyo markets, 8. *See also* markets
tools, technical analysis
  charts, 170-174
  drawing channels/trend lines, 175-177
  indicators/oscillators, 163-170
TPL (Total Profit & Loss), 122
trade balance, 136-137

FINANCIAL TIMES

In an increasingly competitive world, it is quality
of thinking that gives an edge—an idea that opens new
doors, a technique that solves a problem, or an insight
that simply helps make sense of it all.

We work with leading authors in the various arenas
of business and finance to bring cutting-edge thinking
and best-learning practices to a global market.

It is our goal to create world-class print publications
and electronic products that give readers
knowledge and understanding that can then be
applied, whether studying or at work.

To find out more about our business
products, you can visit us at www.ftpress.com.